FILM PRODUCTION

THE COMPLETE
UNCENSORED
GUIDE TO
INDEPENDENT
FILMMAKING

For Mom

FILM PRODUCTION

THE COMPLETE UNCENSORED GUIDE TO INDEPENDENT FILMMAKING

GREG MERRITT

LONE EAGLE PUBLISHING CO.™
1024 North Orange Drive
Hollywood, California 90038
Phone 323.308.3400 or 800.815.0503
A division of IFILM® Corp., www.ifilm.com

Quotations on pages xi, 58, 114, and 151 are from "Directing The Film" by Eric Sherman (Acrobat Books, 1988). Used by permission of the author.

Printed in the United States of America
Cover design by Lindsay Albert

Library of Congress Cataloging-in-Publication Data
Merritt, Greg, 1965–
      Film production : the complete uncensored guide to filmmaking
/
Greg Merritt.
            p.   cm.
      Includes index.
      ISBN 0-943728-99-1
      1. Motion pictures—Production and direction.   2. Low budget motion pictures. I. Title.
      PN1995.9.P7M43   1998
      791.43'0233—dc21   97-25549
                                                          CIP

IFILM® is a registered trademark.
Lone Eagle Publishing Company™ is a registered trademark.

CONTENTS

PRODUCTION

POST-PRODUCTION

DISTRIBUTION

POST-POST-PRODUCTION

ACKNOWLEDGMENTS

A heartfelt thanks to the following people: Ken Nunney, Samuel Ameen, Kate Kennedy, Tracy Curtis, Cecil Gentry, Siena Goines, Thom Hunt, Megan Edwards, Seth Peterson, Dirk Wright, Todd Wesson, Walter Powell, the rest of the *Show and Tell* cast and crew; Robert Greenwald, Martin Scorsese, Jim Jarmusch, Paul Schrader, Akira Kurosawa, Sergio Leone, Rod Serling, Roger Ebert, Gene Siskel, Danny Peary, Frederick S. Clarke, Miss Pittinger, Charles Mitchell, Arnold Lipkind, James Hosney; everyone else who helped, taught or inspired me; Donald and Rose Merritt, the Carricos (Laurie, John, Dylan, Lowell) and Dave; the folks at Lone Eagle Publishing; and LaVonya Sturges.

INTRODUCTION

"The last thing in the world to be worried about is how to make the picture. After the money, the most important thing to worry about is the erection you get of wanting to make a film, a certain film, and nothing will stop you."

—*Samuel Fuller*

Sam Fuller, notoriously macho independent director of such B-movie classics as *The Naked Kiss* (1964), may have overstated the case (and in a sexist manner), but he's correct in pegging what—let's just call "enthusiasm"—as the most important ingredient in filmmaking.

That said, these pages are not filled with cheerleading. Too much of what passes for movie-making instruction is either an empty pep talk or a collection of impractical generalities. This book aims to cut through the fluff and provide you with real-world facts about all aspects of creating and selling a motion picture outside of the Hollywood studios. It is mostly straightforward and proven advice for saving you time, money and sanity.

Despite the attention in recent years heaped upon trend-setting events like the Sundance Film Festival and maverick success stories like Quentin Tarantino, the nuts and bolts of producing an independent feature are anything but glamorous; often, the facts are downright gruesome. Credit card financing and crew mutinies may make for interesting stories, but in reality, much of the sweat and toil of making a motion picture on a shoestring is just that: sweat and toil on a shoestring.

Independent filmmaking is a brutal racket. You may slog away for years, writing, financing and shooting your movie, making it exactly as you dreamed. Still, the odds are that not only will it never be appreciated but probably only a very few people will ever even have the opportunity to appreciate it. In today's crowded fight for theatrical distribution, the sad but most likely scenario is that no one besides your family and friends (and perhaps a few dozen cinema gatekeepers) will view your creation.

Before that sobering thought sinks in, you should know that the actual making of a movie is (usually) not such a bad experience. Independent filmmaking, even with a budget scrounged entirely from your meager savings, should be fun. Except for the lack of a steady pay check, it sure beats a real job. The utter freedom of answering to no one while capturing your dream with light and mirrors on celluloid is a thrill few humans get to experience. (Even most outrageously-compensated Hollywood directors never know this feeling.) Low-budget movie production is not glamorous, but, even when it should be torture because of the long hours or enormous hassles or great personal expense, it still often feels like a blast.

Back to Sam Fuller. Yes, enthusiasm and persistence and an overwhelming urge for creating a significant motion picture really do matter more than anything. But, you're not going to find these things in a book. Instead, you've got to have a burning desire right down to the marrow of your bones. Only then will you be fully able to convince investors and actors and crew members and distributors and all the entertainment angels to believe in your film with the passion everyone will need to have to get it done and get it done right. Only then will you be able to plow through all the money problems and people problems and more money problems to make a successful movie against all the seemingly insurmountable odds.

* * *

Some of the greatest motion pictures in history were created without the aid of major Hollywood studios and on meager budgets. Early classics such as Robert Flaherty's ground-breaking documentary, *Nanook of the North* (1922), and the self-financed comedy features of Harold Lloyd were films that, today, would be referred to as "indies." Furthermore, in an ironic twist of history, the forerunners of today's Hollywood studios were the original independents—formed to combat the patent trust of Thomas Edison and compatriots.

But these once-independent production companies soon became all-powerful entertainment factories. During the 1930s and 1940s, the studios dominated the industry, controlling film exhibition as well as production. Plenty of cheap B-movies were made during this era, but most of them (such as Edgar Ulmer's classic *Detour* (1946), shot in six days on six sets) were still by-products of the system, frequently made by small "Poverty Row" studios like Monogram or Republic. Truly independent films, such as the avant-garde work of Maya Deren and the all-black no-budget flicks of directors like Oscar Micheaux and Spencer Williams, went virtually unacknowledged.

In the late '40s and early '50s, the Supreme Court handed down a series of consent decrees that broke up the monopoly of the film studios, freeing theaters to play what they choose. Autonomy in financing and production resulted in several semi-indie classics, including *The African Queen* (1951), *On The Waterfront* (1954) and *Twelve Angry Men* (1957).

The death of the studio system also led to the careers of bargain basement indie "auteurs" like Ed Wood, whose laughably lame flicks include *Plan 9 From Outer Space* (1956); Russ Meyer who served up soft-core porn like *The Immortal Mr. Teas* (1959); and Roger Corman, whose entertaining *The Little Shop of Horrors* (1960) was shot in only two days (breaking his own five-day record for *Bucket of Blood*, 1959).

Around this time, in France, a few young intellectuals dropped the cinema journals they wrote for, picked up cameras and led a filmmaking revolution that would rock art houses worldwide. Thus began the French New Wave. With the skimpiest of budgets, movies like Jean-Luc Godard's neo-gangster *Breathless* (1959), François Truffaut's humanistic *The 400 Blows*, (1959) and Alain Resnais' experiment in memory, *Hiroshima, Mon Amour* (1959), became spellbinding masterpieces. Using such techniques as improvised dialogue, stark documentary-style camera work, stock footage and jump-cut editing, these films flaunted and subverted cinema conventions. In a fury of productivity in the early '60s, the New Wave directors managed—by concentrating on style and stories—to turn their lack of substantial budgets into artistic strengths. And the world took notice.

Inspired by the celluloid revolution in Europe, American artists of all stripes began filming the stories that mainstream Hollywood refused to touch. Thus began a remarkable period of cinematic innovation. From the mid-'60s through the '70s, one can plot a course in the American indie scene of some of the most original and influential movies of all time: Samuel Fuller's tough-as-nails *The Naked Kiss* (1965); George Romero's cult horror phenomenon, *Night of the Living Dead* (1968); *Easy Rider* (1969), Dennis Hopper's mega-successful road trip; Melvin Van Peebles' radical blaxploitation genesis, *Sweet Sweetback's Baadasssss Song* (1971); the porno that launched an industry, Gerald Damiano's *Deep Throat* (1972); John Waters' $12,000 trash legend, *Pink Flamingos* (1972); *Mean Streets* (1973), Martin Scorsese's first gangster slice-of-life (featuring relative newcomer Robert De Niro); indie legend John Cassavetes' emotion-wrenched *A Woman Under the Influence* (1974); Barbara Kopple's harrowing documentary, *Harlan County, U.S.A.* (1976); David Lynch's first and weirdest, *Eraserhead* (1978); and John Carpenter's mega-successful fright-fest, *Halloween* (1978).

By the 1980s, enough substantial American films were being made outside of the traditional Hollywood studio system to establish the catchword "independent" as a genre unto itself, with festivals and film markets and a selective audience. At the beginning of the decade, John Sayles made the ensemble piece *Return of the Secaucus 7* (1980) with his own $60,000. A host of talented directors followed a similar path. Influential films made during this decade include: Louis Malle's one location, two-actor conversation, *My Dinner with Andre* (1981); Joel Cohen's twisting film noir, *Blood Simple* (1985); Jim Jarmusch's laid-back *Stranger than Paradise* (1984); Spike Lee's low-budget comedy hit *She's Gotta Have It* (1986); and Errol Morris' stylized documentary, *The Thin Blue Line* (1988). The decade was topped off by Steven Soderbergh's box office sensation, *sex, lies and videotape* (1989), which firmly established the independent film scene (and Sundance in particular) as a key proving ground for mainstream success.

The 1990s have brought us Richard Linklater's $23,000 structural chain letter, *Slacker* (1991); Quentin Tarantino's brutal heist-gone-wrong *Reservoir Dogs* (1992); Carl Franklin's crime sojourn, *One False Move* (1991); Robert Rodriguez's $7,000 actioner, *El Mariachi* (1993); Steve James, Frederick Marx and Peter Gilbert's unforgettable documentary, *Hoop Dreams* (1994); Kevin Smith's $27,000 grunge comedy, *Clerks* (1994); Mike Figgis' Oscar-winning plunge, *Leaving Las Vegas* (1995); Billy Bob Thornton's Southern character study, *Sling Blade* (1996); and a host of other innovative, influential, independent films.

If you view the motion pictures listed here, you'll understand that cinema need not be stifled by meager budgets, a lack of studio input or the unease of not knowing if your labor of love will ever see the dark of a movie theater. In fact, often these supposed shortcomings can be artistically liberating. Likewise, you'll see in these indies that making a very good motion picture does not require big name stars in front of the lens or award-winning artists behind it. Nor do you have to have the best equipment or facilities or locations or costumes or any other material things. After studying these movies, you'll realize that the qualities shared by the best of them are a great **story** and an original directorial **vision**. And a story and a vision—the two most important factors in your filmmaking success—don't have to cost you a single dime.

* * *

Let's get a few things straight. This book is about **independent** filmmaking. Such a term is tricky to define when confused with **independent studio** efforts like Hemdale's *Platoon* (1986) and Miramax's *Pulp Fiction* (1994), but, for our purposes, an independent film can most simply be defined as: a movie financed and produced outside of the studio system (including the independent studio system).

The term **low-budget** is also tossed around on these pages. For our purposes, this is defined as a movie made for less than $500,000. Additionally, **micro-budget** means any movie made for less than $150,000.

Although there is a wealth of information on guerilla filmmaking to follow, most of this book will apply to ALL independent films, regardless of budget. After all, a $20,000 and a $2 million production may seem miles apart when you're strapped with the smaller budget, but even seven digits is spare change in these days of $100+ million studio pictures. All independent films need to pinch pennies.

This book is not specifically about **movies shot on video** and yet what follows can serve as a manual for such productions. Feature films with a strong hook can be made with a broadcast-quality video camera, finished for less than $30,000 (sometimes for less than $2,000!) and sold to video companies. Although such productions are not our principal focus, videographers can benefit from virtually all the information within these pages (facts on film labs and film stock excepted). Only when it comes to distribution will most videomakers take a wholly different path, directly approaching video distributors for a sale. By the way, features can be shot on video and then transferred to 35mm film. Increasingly popular with documentaries since *Hoop Dreams* was completed this way, fiction features are now flirting with this option as well.

Though our attention is primarily on narrative films, documentarians should not feel ignored. These pages do not address the specific techniques of making **documentaries**, such as researching, interviewing and compiling archival footage, but documentary directors and producers can apply, word-for-word, most of the pre- and post-production advice. Furthermore, because nearly all nonexploitation independents travel the same route, the section entitled "DISTRIBUTION" presents a strategy for any festival-bound film.

At first glance, this book may appear to be a bit snobbish: it does, after all, address primarily festival-quality material and seems to neglect tried-and-true **exploitation** genres such as action, soft-core porn, martial arts and horror. Don't worry. The land of independent distribution—home to the ultimate breast-man Russ Meyer and rubber monster king Roger Corman—has always been an acceptable refuge for the lepers of the movie world. Four of the most successful nonstudio flicks of all time are in the horror genre: *Night of the Living Dead* (1968), *Halloween* (1978), *Friday the 13th* (1980) and *The Texas Chainsaw Massacre* (1974). The latter actually played in the Director's Fortnight of the 1976 Cannes Film Festival. The ultimate trash-a-thon, *Pink Flamingos*, notorious for the 300-pound transvestite Divine snacking on dog excrement, made millions on the midnight movie circuit. The independently-produced *Billy Jack* (1971) and *Walking Tall* (1973) were blockbuster nights-at-the-fights. And sex always sells. The hard-core pornographic *Deep Throat* is arguably the most successful motion picture ever made, when considering expenses to returns.

Welcome, unwashed and unwanted, to the film orphanage that is independent cinema. Most of this book will apply to you until you reach distribution. With very few exceptions, exploitation pictures will not play at festivals. Some may make it into theaters, but the vast majority will travel straight to (exploitation) video distributors and cable television. (Note that the movies listed in the preceding paragraph were all huge theatrical successes but they were released between 1968 and 1979. VCRs and cable TV forever changed the world of low-budget gore, tits and kicks.)

Finally, there is no doubt that this book is aimed primarily at feature-length motion pictures. **Short films** are always low-budget and are nearly always independent, narrative and prime festival material—but everyone slights shorts. Actually, as with the exploitation category, everything that follows is applicable to shorts (on a smaller financial scale, of course) until you get to distribution. Then the question becomes "What distribution?" Besides a few specialized TV channels and the occasional compilation screening, options for making money from shorts are small indeed.

* * *

This book is addressed to "you" in a second-person sense—as a filmmaker endeavoring to make a feature-length motion picture. For our purposes, **filmmaker** means **director**. To a degree, it also means **producer** or **principal investor**. As we'll get to in the next section, you may also be the **screenwriter**. Of course, no one checked your ID when you opened the cover. You may be all or none of these things. Maybe you're an actor, an editor, a cinematographer. Maybe you occupy some other equally important position. Perhaps you're just a curious civilian who wants to learn the real truth about making movies. Whatever. When you read "you," think of yourself as the director/producer.

One other matter of semantics. As you may already have noticed, this book refers to directors in conjunction with their films, almost always at the expense of anyone else. This is done not out of blind adherence to the auteur theory of "director as author." And it is certainly not intended to slight the writers, actors, producers, cinematographers, production designers, editors, composers and many other talented people involved in motion picture production (and who often play a more crucial role in a completed film's success than the director). It is merely shorthand. Never lose sight of the fact that making a movie is a collaborative art. To be successful, a film production typically requires the skills of dozens of hard-working individuals striving towards the same goal.

* * *

On to the naked facts of independent filmmaking. You may want to give yourself that pep talk now. What follows is often uninspiring, sometimes unpleasant and almost never glamorous, but what else could it be when you're trying to make a successful work of commercial art with a couple dozen people and a lot of expensive equipment while constricted by the slimmest of budgets, and you're competing for attention against thousands of others trying to do the same damn thing. Yes, it'll be brutal. But it should also be a blast.

PRE-PREPRODUCTION

1/SCRIPT

The script is the single most important component in your film. It's the foundation on which everything is built: financing, acting, locations, design, cinematic style, audience identification . . . everything. You cannot make a great movie with anything less than a great script.

The script is all the more crucial for the independent filmmaker. Without explosions or familiar faces or all the tinsel that millions of dollars can add to the screen to distract the audience, your screenplay will be nearly naked. Weak stories, hackneyed characters and lame dialogue stand out in low-budget features for all to see and to cringe at. In a defenseless indie, even relatively minor writing flaws can irritate viewers. On the other hand, if your script is well-written, void of all the noise and stars and flash, it'll be allowed to truly shine. Witness the independent and "indie studio" flicks winning screenwriting Academy Awards in the 1990s, including *Pulp Fiction*, *The Usual Suspects* and *Sling Blade*.

In the beginning, everything is equal. Big-budget action pictures or low-budget character dramas are born from screenplays: a hundred or so white pages and some black ink. Take advantage of the level playing field while it's there. Remember: it costs virtually nothing to write a good script, and yet it is the most important factor in the success or failure of your motion picture. In addition to the obvious creative benefits, a great script serves as a blueprint that makes everything else easier, including financing, casting, assembling a crew and directing.

A final word on the importance of words: Don't convince yourself that you can fix a less-than-satisfactory script once cameras are rolling. Before production begins, do not be satisfied with anything less than a great screenplay.

WRITERS

It seems like everyone with even a passing interest in the film business has written a screenplay. But suffer through a few of these and you'll see that completing a good (let alone great) script is much more difficult than merely calling yourself a screenwriter. Few scripts possess the power to move; few cry out to be turned into moving pictures; few can entertain from "Fade in" to "Fade out." If and when you find one that accomplishes all of these things and that can be shot within the confines of your budget, pounce on it. It's a rare jewel indeed.

Script prices vary from zero to millions. Minimum compensation for features budgeted at less than $2.5 million, set by the Writers Guild of America (WGA), is more than $25,000, plus contributions to the guild's pension and health funds. If your budget is seven figures, this may be relevant. But the fact is, most writers of shoestring indies aren't in the WGA (you only become a member by first selling a script to a Guild signatory) and, even if they are, minimum rates can be easily sidestepped.

Try to get a screenplay for little or no money up-front. Offer as payment a "written by" credit, the thrill of having writing produced and some **profit points** (a percentage share of any potential profits). If that doesn't do it, typical fees are one to two percent of the budget up-front and one to two percent when the film goes into production.

Literary properties, such as books, stage plays, magazine articles, etc., that you would like to adapt into a screenplay must be **optioned** (contractually "picked up," with the right to purchase later) from whomever has retained the copyright (usually the author or his agent). For books, the copyright is listed on back of the title page. Scripts, too, can be optioned and used as part of your investment package and to attract name actors as you seek financing. Option agreements are typically in effect for one to two years, after which they can be extended.

Well-known properties and writers will most probably be out of your price range, but the little-known work of a little-known author often can be optioned for a paltry sum (one dollar is the no-budget standard), with the hope of a bigger payday in the future. The contract should contain a literary purchase agreement to go into effect if and when your movie begins production. This usually includes such elements as:

- rights to the title, plot, theme, and characters;
- permission to use the property in various mediums (film, TV, video, etc.);
- permission to make changes to the writing;
- permission to advertise and market the material as a film.

Fees for purchasing vary greatly (up to the millions), but you may be able to get an unknown property for a few thousand dollars. Sometimes, deals can be swung with just the lure of profit participation.

You may need to hire a screenwriter to adapt an optioned property for the screen, to turn an idea into a script or to rewrite a screenplay. Recommendations and sample scripts are the best methods for discerning a talented writer (emphasis on *talented*). Get someone with obvious abilities for the style of story you want to tell. It's sad but true: unproduced scribes desperate for a first screen credit will often toil away for little or no money.

Work closely with the writer to be certain the finished screenplay fits your needs, your style and your budget. Value the creative process enough to give this person latitude when writing, but when he hands you his completed draft, read it carefully and make detailed notes. Do not sign off on a final draft unless you are one hundred percent ecstatic about it. Never forget how important the script is. If it's just not happening, it may be time to look for another writer.

Often, with independent films, you (the director and/or producer) will also be the screenwriter. It'll be your written story that you translate into pictures and spoken words. From hereon, our discussion of screenwriting is addressed to you as the writer, but the same rules apply whether you're penning a script or analyzing the work of someone else.

IDEA

Screenwriting 101: Film is a marketing industry. Pound this mantra into your head. From the very beginning, you should be fully aware of this fact; and you should keep these words echoing in your skull every step of the way. How can you sell your movie to investors, distributors, ticket buyers? Of course, this sort of thinking is often blamed for much of the typical studio fare: the "high concept" effluvia, the halfhearted sequel, the remake of a lame TV sitcom. But, knowing how you'll sell your film doesn't mean you have to pander to the lowest IQs of the widest possible audience. You may very well plan to market your movie as a revolutionary farce or a quirky romance, but know where you're going before beginning your journey. Film is a marketing industry.

When it comes to marketing films, the idea is paramount. Whether people are contemplating investing in it, distributing it or shelling out cash to see it, the first thing they want to know is: "What's it about?" Well, you had better be able to explain your story compellingly in three lines or less. Ask yourself:

- What will get people interested?

- What makes your idea different from the standard Hollywood concepts?

- What will make your future film stand apart from last year's independent releases?

Consider the film festival break-out movies of the recent past. *Stranger than Paradise* (1984) has a compelling yet economical style comprised of long, wide shots that envelope its sparse dialogue and subdued plotting. *Slacker* (1991), in addition to coining a generational term, has a unique (and money-saving) structure of short scenes with different characters, thus allowing the camera to seemingly wander around Austin, Texas. *Reservoir Dogs* (1992) has an in-your-face style, with a jumbled framework, brazen dialogue and surprising bursts of ultra-violence. *Clerks* (1994), buoyed by genuinely funny dialogue, manages to make its cheap look and convenience store location part of its charm.

Come to the table with something innovative: topic, setting, dialogue, structure, characters, theme, filmic style. At the very least, reinterpret something old. But do not try to steal from the current festival darling: this year's sensation is next year's old news.

Making an independent film will present a seemingly endless barrage of obstacles. Your one true advantage over cushier entertainment occupations will be the wealth of creative freedom afforded you. Utilize this to its fullest: Make the movie that only you, of all the potential filmmakers in the world, can make. Having said that, don't get caught up doing something new just for the sake of doing something new. Too many "artists" convince themselves they'll soon be revolutionizing the cinema or ushering in the new "New Wave." Most often what they usher in is pretentious filmmaking. Be original, but, as in any art form, master the basics before making the masterpiece.

Furthermore, as an almost-but-not-quite general rule, all creative decisions should, first and foremost, serve your story. In the vast majority of cases, if something runs counter to or distracts from your storytelling, it doesn't belong in your script. For example, Gus Van Sant's *My Own Private Idaho* would be a better picture without occasionally veering off into Shakespearian language and characters. Yes, it's different, but it's also distracting.

Screenwriting 102: Stories should say something. A message, in the form of a **theme**, should be contained in your screenplay. However, do not have a character bluntly state the lesson learned. The message should be just below the surface where it can become apparent, with minimal analysis. Your script's theme will, in essence, be your statement about the human condition. Don't let this intimidate you. Just know that your motion picture should be about an idea and this idea should be more than just a device to drive the plot. It should be a way of telling the audience something it needs to hear, something they can take home when they wonder out of the theater.

STRUCTURE

Screenwriting books, courses and seminars promise to unlock the innermost mysteries of the **three-act structure** and launch one towards scriptwriting success. Despite the relentless sales pitch, the three-act structure is not a magic formula; it's just basic drama. Your script should have three underlying sections, called **acts**: a beginning (approximately the first thirty pages), a middle (the next fifty-five or more pages) and an end (the final fifteen to twenty-five pages).

Act One introduces the characters, the situation and a dilemma that forces the main character (protagonist) to take action. The

7

dilemma is the "hook" and it should be compelling enough to sustain the viewer's interest throughout. It's your principal job within the first half of the first act to grab the audience; it's your job for the rest of the script to hold them.

Act Two builds obstacles that prevent the protagonist from solving his dilemma; in essence, escalating the stakes of the story. Most script problems materialize in the middle. Therefore, stay focused on making elements progressively more difficult for your protagonist. This is true whether the dilemma is subtle (i.e., a character deciding if he should stay with his lover) or overt (i.e., the hero battling giant blood-sucking spiders).

Act Three resolves the dilemma and wraps up elements in a satisfying manner (which is not necessarily "happily"). When movies fall apart at the end, it is either because they dawdle (do not introduce principal characters or new issues in act three) or because an event happens that doesn't ring true with the buildup of the first two acts.

Studio story analysts and screenwriting lecturers often become so enamored by structure that they see little else. The truth is that every screenplay needs a beginning, a middle and an end, but there are more crucial components than having a **plot point** (the revealing of a crucial development) fall on a specific page. In fact, non-studio films sometimes achieve a greater effect by breaking these strict rules of structure and surprising the audience precisely because typical Hollywood fare has conditioned us to anticipate a twist only at specific times. Witness *The Crying Game* (1992), which springs its big twist (and biggest dilemma) in the middle of act two. Furthermore, what is so striking about a movie like *Slacker* is that it has no trace of a three-act structure, but instead, it meanders relentlessly, as befits its aimless characters. The same is true of *Twenty Bucks* (1993), which follows a twenty dollar bill as it weaves in and out of various lives. Most stories should not be so spineless. Most scripts should have three acts. Still, do not become a slave to the minutiae of so-called structure rules.

Branching off from the main plot are **subplots**. These are not mandatory but are generally a welcome addition. By highlighting emotional elements in your movie, they can be even more compelling than the main plot. Often, a subplot is the love story. In most cases, a subplot should come with its own set of complications and have a beginning, middle and end.

Conflict is the essence of all dramatic writing—it's what really makes a script work. Conflict begets **tension** and it is what drives your movie forward. This is as true for a romantic comedy as it is for a thriller. And . . . it's always true. Measures of conflict and tension will enliven even the most apparently innocent scene. People disagreeing, however slightly, is almost always more engrossing than people agreeing. When creating conflict, first establish what each main character wants. You cannot expect conflict to rise around someone who has no desires. Next, present barriers to a character (i.e., people, circumstances, etc.), causing him to struggle to overcome them.

The most crucial thing for the writer and director to have is an overall vision of the story/film. **Cohesion** comes about when you have such a vision. In most cases, the tone of your script should remain consistent throughout. But more than that, every scene, every character and every action should work together towards the same goal. If you don't have a master plan, you'll tend to insert elements that may be great by themselves but are merely distracting when part of the whole (i.e., Falstaff in *My Own Private Idaho*). By the way, cohesion does not mean that all elements must advance the plot by leaps and bounds. Quite the contrary. If you have an overall vision, you'll know when to let up on the tension; you'll know when a diversion will work to your advantage; and you'll know when it will not.

Methods for adding to script cohesion include recurring **motifs** (i.e., repeating images, rhythms, sounds). They may or may not be symbols, but they should help the audience focus on certain key story elements. As an example, *Blue Velvet* (1986) has an insect motif. From the idea to the musical score, be aware of motifs that you can connect throughout. **Foreshadowing** and **payoff** refer to a visual clue or spoken line that returns later. The payoff is generally greater if the item's meaning (when foreshadowed) is not readily apparent. This tool is useful for keeping the audience involved, as well as for uniting diverse sections of a film. *Drugstore Cowboy* (1989) has foreshadowing and payoff through its hat-on-the-bed motif and via the circumstances of the first shot only becoming clear at the conclusion.

When it comes to structure and cohesion, one thing that separates great scripts from weak ones is strong, crisp **transitions**. Try to find a creative way to connect the end of one scene with the

9

beginning of another. *Pulp Fiction,* with its overlapping dialogue and nonlinear framework, has great transitions throughout. In this vein, don't telegraph a new setting. It's almost always more effective if someone doesn't let us know where they're going next. (We'll see it soon enough.) While you're hunched over your script, never forget how powerful and immediate the visuals of cinema are. In an instant, a picture will tell us as much about a new scene as a character could in a thousand words.

A cohesive big-picture vision often implants itself on a film during the rewriting process. When editing a script, integrate scenes and characters to serve your overall purpose. Chop out those that aren't working towards the greater goal. A bit of rewriting advice: When in doubt, cut it out.

CHARACTER

The importance of fresh, dimensional characters cannot be overemphasized. What we remember most from movies is almost always the interesting people we meet, not the specific machinations of the plot. Sometimes this is because of the actor's performance, but just as often, it's because the characters are so striking and unique. Independent films often contain some of the screen's most memorable characters because they're written to be fresh and unpredictable and to contrast with the people found in standard Hollywood movies. You can see such vivid characters in indies like: *She's Gotta Have It, Heathers, Leaving Las Vegas,* and *Sling Blade.* Surprise us. Go against clichés. Create new people.

You must know your characters. Before you begin writing your script, you may want to create a personal history or list of traits for each main role. Consult this whenever your characters need to speak or act; it will help you grasp their tendencies, determine where they're coming from and where they're going and differentiate them from each other.

All significant characters should have something at stake and something they want. Knowing these will bring their **motivation(s)** into focus. Characters may not always be conscious of their own needs, and flawed characters can lose sight of their overall goals (causing motivations to change from moment to moment). However, you as the writer should never lose sight of them. Ask yourself what your characters want in each scene. More than any other factor, the answer will help determine what they do and say.

A character's true nature is exposed through conflict. Opposing desires will collide with the greatest impact. In order to properly heighten tension, the antagonist should be at least equally as strong as the protagonist. Strong villains are the key element in many stories.

A popular method of connecting audience members to the people on the screen is to make the characters sympathetic. The studios often interpret this to mean that the protagonist should be an amiable, upstanding citizen. For our more subversive purposes of making a great independent film, let's just say that even if your character is despicable, it's helpful (but not mandatory) if he has something we can relate to: a glint of kindness, a foible, a sense of humor—any trait that feels familiar. (Superman has Kryptonite, after all, and his weakness around green rocks is his most compelling quality.) As Shakespeare knew so well, it is people's flaws that make them intriguing.

Well-developed characters should experience a change, great or small, through the course of your story. This means that forces will come to weigh on them and/or other characters will affect them so that their views are altered and they change their ways. This overall growth is called a **character arc** and it can be extreme or subtle. It's frequently interconnected with your script's theme. Characters don't have to experience an arc, but it is advantageous if at least your protagonist learns some kind of lesson along the way.

DIALOGUE

Character traits and **motivations** (covered in the previous section) are key factors in determining what a character says and how he says it. Another is the character's **emotional state**. Be aware of each character's emotions at all times because people speak differently depending on what they're feeling—and what they're feeling can change from moment to moment.

Generally, you should give each of your main characters a **distinctive voice**. Education, class and geographic region are three such qualifiers for speech. *Sling Blade* is an excellent example of differentiated dialogue, even among poor people in the South; *The Usual Suspects* (1995) has several similar characters (male criminals) but each speaks in his own distinct manner. A good method for achieving this is to read a character's lines alone, concentrating on just that person's particular idioms, syntax, slang, repeating words

11

and phrases. Make sure the elements that make a character unique are not shared by another.

What a character says is not as important as how he says it and what he doesn't say. For this reason, dialogue should never be *on the nose*, as in: "I hate him because he reminds me of my father." (This character probably wouldn't want to talk about dear old dad at all.) The really important issues will be alluded to or, better yet, they'll come out through character actions and reactions. In a similar vein, try not to let dialogue substitute for the visual image. If you can show something through action (maybe just a seemingly insignificant look), it is almost always the most efficient method of getting information across.

Basic dialogue advice suggests keeping passages short. Although this is a valid recommendation, there are notable exceptions. *Reservoir Dogs*, for example, has numerous chunks of dialogue that last a half-page or more. *Sling Blade* has a page-eating speech near the beginning (when Carl tells his criminal history). So, you can ignore this rule for effect, but for the most part, your film will move faster with shorter, punchier speeches. Also, less experienced actors (usually, the type who work in low-budget movies) can more easily master brief passages.

To test your dialogue, read it out loud. Words often have an entirely different effect (or lack of effect) when spoken. It's even better to get someone else or several someone elses (ideally, actors) to read your script to you. When you hear the dialogue during rehearsals, don't be afraid to change things that don't sound right or that don't fit the voice or abilities of the performer. Be sure to get the dialogue worked out before going into production . . . but don't be afraid to change it then, either.

LOW-BUDGET RULES
Because one of the most important qualities in any low-budget screenplay is, by definition, its ability to be produced on a low budget, you must think of how to minimize money constraints during the writing process. Needless to say, it'll be more difficult to

remove an explosion or high-rent location once the movie is in production. Avoid such problems by not writing them into the script.

When considering budgetary constraints, use the following general guidelines (but remember, there are exceptions to every coupon-clipping tip):

- The fewer locations, the better.

- Each location should be cheaply available and easily accessible. (Even if all sites are free, the time spent moving can add to your budget.) By the way, limiting the number of locations is directly opposite of the philosophy held by large budget productions, which want to maximize scenic locales to keep audiences entertained.

- The smaller the cast, the better. Even if actors work for free, you'll still have the expense of feeding them (a major cost). Creativity can go a long way: *Citizen Kane* (1941), to name one lofty example, gives the feeling of crowds when, in reality, there are just a few people present.

- Steer clear of period, science fiction and fantasy costumes and decor. Unless the cast and locations are kept to a bare minimum, or you're making a broad spoof in which poverty is part of the humor (à la the period *Monty Python and the Holy Grail* [1975] or the sci-fi *Dark Star* [1974]), the design and clothing of past or future times is difficult to pull off without substantial funds.

- Avoid complex stunts. Don't write in any action that requires a union stunt person (the words "union" and "low-budget" almost never go together). The liability insurance alone could do you in.

- Avoid special effects (FX). Blank gunshots and some gruesome makeup can be managed safely and cheaply, but most other FX can't. (See "MAKING A MOVIE: Special Effects & Stunts.") Events such as fires and car crashes might seem relatively cheap to stage, but for safety reasons, you'll be required to have experts and emergency technicians on-set while you film.

- Prohibitively expensive events can sometimes be staged off-screen to greater dramatic effect. (Perhaps you can show the *reaction* of an observer as an explosion or car crash is heard.) Post-production sounds are easy and cheap.

- Don't write into the script extreme weather conditions (i.e., heavy rain, snow, etc.) unless they are shot through a window during interior scenes. Staging shots in extreme weather (real or fake) is difficult and can cause budget-busting problems for a limited crew with limited equipment.

- Casting young children (but not teenagers, for whom you can cast legal adult actors, aged eighteen or older) can create a hailstorm of work restrictions and education requirements (see "CAST: Minors"). If possible, avoid making child roles a primary focus of your script.

- Be creative, be frugal and plan ahead.

BLOOD, SEX & ACTION

Blood, sex and action ruled the land of low-budget independents during the age of drive-ins and midnight cult movies. Today, important film festivals (like Sundance) and the critical press reign supreme, and there are two schools of thought on exploitation.

The first says that traditional exploitation elements will kill your film's chances of being accepted into major film festivals and of reaching the independent big-time. *Reservoir Dogs* and *El Mariachi* aside, there is some truth to this. The indie scene has turned away from gratuitous bloodletting, nude bimbos, car chases and the like . . . unless they're done in an artful way. The second school of thought says that exploitation elements may provide a financial safety net.

Consider this: there were nearly 800 submissions to Sundance 1997 and only thirty-six were shown in the dramatic film categories (less than one in twenty!). Furthermore, of those thirty-six, most will never be theatrically distributed. The odds are daunting. So, as a fallback position, in case your dream project isn't accepted to Sundance, or if Miramax doesn't call, you possibly still can collect money by making a sale to a video label (especially a foreign label)—if your film contains some exploitation elements. Such a deal may not sound very optimistic but it can be great news if you're maxed-out on credit cards or you're contemplating a job under the golden arches. And, the fact is, the direct-to-video market cares less about artistic, inventive and quirky material and more about gore, tits and explosions. They also like at least one recognizable name they can sell (see "CAST: Recognizable Names").

Therefore, consider a bit of exploitation in your artistic, inventive, quirky independent feature. Just consider it. If it doesn't work for your story don't force it. *Clerks* was not going to be distributed in European video stores if it hadn't been the hit of Sundance 1994, and the addition of blood, sex and convenience store action were not going to change that. Still, some movies can squeeze such elements in and they may provide the safety net needed in this very risky world of independent film production.

SHOOTING SCRIPT

As the director, you write the shooting script. This is your playbook for turning the writer's screenplay into your film. In the shooting script, how each dialogue passage and action sequence will be covered is noted (see "DIRECTING A MOVIE: Coverage"). Shots are numbered.

It is important that you work on the shooting script as soon as possible. Although it will undergo many changes, including during production, the shooting script is an important document for preproduction when it comes to elements such as scheduling, hiring the crew, establishing equipment needs and setting the budget.

Just as the screenwriter must be aware of costs when writing the script, the director should be conscious of his budget when preparing his coverage. A few suggestions:

- Limit complicated camera setups and dolly moves. Some elaborate movements can easily take half a day to shoot. If you're planning a long dolly shot, make sure it covers a significant amount of script or that you can make up the time elsewhere.

- Generally, the closer your coverage, the easier it is to light. Close-ups can often be lit in less than fifteen minutes. Conversely, setting up a wide shot can take hours. Wide interior shots should usually be **masters** (shots that cover a lot of script, usually followed by closer coverage).

- Be aware of what equipment your budget will allow. Crane shots, multi-camera coverage, aerial footage and distorting lenses may be cost prohibitive. Some luxuries can be squeezed into budgets by renting (or borrowing) the equipment for only a day, but you'll need to consider this when penning your shooting script and setting up the schedule.

- Avoid optical effects, such as slow-motion, freeze frames, transitional wipes, etc., which must be done by optical houses and can be prohibitively expensive.

- Consider **stock footage**. It can be a budget savior. Crowd scenes, special effects, natural wonders—almost anything and everything—can be obtained from stock houses for relatively little cost when compared to shooting them. You may be able to afford helicopter shots of that erupting volcano after all.

Keep the budget in mind when writing your shooting script, but don't sacrifice or greatly compromise your overall vision. Let the cinematographer, producer(s), and other key crew members have input early as to what can and cannot be done with the schedule, budget and crew. If there are complex shots or sequences that you feel are crucial, they can often be squeezed in. Creative things can be accomplished with a lot of planning and ingenuity. Always be realistic, but don't sell your dream short . . . not yet, anyway.

2/MONEY

It's no big secret, of course, that movies, unlike most other art forms, require a significant chunk of money to be created. If you or your family or some very supportive friends can supply the funds to cover your budget, great—you're set. Skip this section and commence preproduction. If not, prepare to grovel and scrounge. Above all else, it's the producer's job to find the dough. Sometimes this takes years and sometimes it requires swallowing pride. If you believe in your vision—really believe in it with all your mind, body and soul—you must be willing to do whatever it takes to capture that vision on film.

INVESTORS
The most important question for many independent producers is: Where do I find people willing to invest in my dream? As difficult as it may be to believe, they're out there. Furthermore, it can actually work to your advantage to be far away from those jaded folks in Hollywood.

Movie-making is enveloped in an aura of glamour. This is true even of guerilla productions, at least in the abstract (when people actually witness a movie shot on a micro-budget, the romance often disappears). So, potential investors are those people with some extra cash who want an invitation into the (supposedly) glamorous world of filmed entertainment.

Gamblers can be found anywhere. Sam Raimi raised funds for his 1982 cult horror flick *The Evil Dead* by shopping a short Super-8 version to doctors and dentists in Michigan. (Living in Detroit, he figured that's where the money was.) Raimi and his partner bought matching briefcases, wore suits and ties and approached potential contributors with the utmost professionalism. People trusted them, bought into their dream and dropped a few thousand dollars into this fun but risky speculation (it eventually paid off). The filmmakers raised $375,000. So there you go. Become a salesperson. Find people with money and approach them with an investment memorandum (details to follow). Like all salespeople, prepare to hear the dreaded "no"-word a few hundred times but always wear a smile and keep charging towards your goal.

Money can come from anywhere. *The Spitfire Grill* raised its $6 million budget from the Sacred Heart League, a Catholic charitable organization which was looking for new ways to generate revenue. Despite the very high risk, the priests poured millions into the collection plate of this New England melodrama starring Ellen Burstyn and shot by an unknown Mississippi company and a first-time director. The shoot even went $1 million over budget. But, hallelujah, the padres' prayers were answered! *Spitfire Grill* played the Sundance Film Festival in 1996, where it was picked up for distribution by Castle Rock for a record $10 million.

There are companies that specialize in **venture capital** (funds invested at considerable risk in potentially high-profit enterprises). You may be able to interest such folks in your project but it's a very tough sell. The risks of independent film production are usually too great. Most venture capitalists won't bet on horses with odds this long.

Another approach is to find someone to find investors for you. This someone should have expertise in film financing and/or connections to the investment community. Many law firms have an attorney in charge of limited partnerships. If one believes in your project, he'll come onboard as your **executive producer**, drafting documents and setting up meetings with potential investors.

So what's in it for them besides a cool screen credit? Depending on how much they raise, they'll get either a very big or a very huge slice of your take. If they find most of the funds, it's common for an attorney/executive producer to contractually take fifty percent of your profits! That's right: he'll get half of your advance, half of your share of the box office, half of your slice of ancillaries, half of your everything. This takes place after all investors have been reimbursed and simultaneous to those same investors pocketing their own huge shares of the profits. Needless to say, it'll be hard for you to see significant money on the back end this way. But, hey, you get to make a movie.

SELLING YOUR DREAM

Selling is all about professionalism. First, form a production company. Choose a name. There, you have a production company. To write and deposit checks under this name, you'll need a business bank account, and to open this, you may need to file and publish a **fictitious business name statement**, but that's about as complicated as it gets.

Next, compile an **investment memorandum package**. Basically, this is a prospectus with a subtle difference (for legal reasons, we won't be calling it a prospectus).

Your investment memorandum package should consist of:

- The **screenplay** and a script **synopsis** (one to two pages).

- Your film's **budget** (as detailed as possible).

- **Résumés or biographies** for such talent as the director, writer, producer, cinematographer and any other crew people with impressive credits, as well as any notable actors who may have signed on.

  NOTE: Getting an actor with a recognizable name to commit early is the Number One factor in attracting money (see "CAST: Recognizable Names").

- **Reels** (compilation videos consisting of the best scenes and shots from various projects) of the director and cinematographer, and sometimes the production designer, editor, or actor(s) (if they have impressive credits). If neither you nor the cinematographer have sufficient experience, don't include any reels. But if you do, bring them on. Investors can be easily impressed by flashy footage.

- **Anything helpful** that will shine a positive light on your investment opportunity: beneficial articles on film financing; 8x10 photos of your actors; stills from other productions which your crew members worked on; artwork, storyboards, or mock advertising for your future blockbuster; video profiles of cast and crew . . . if it helps the cause and you can afford it, include it in your package.

The **investment memorandum** itself is a document consisting of information that will assist the investor in making an intelligent decision about whether or not to back your dream. It should sell the strengths of your film, compare it to other successful independent fare and generally paint a rosy picture.

You must also, by law, present the negative side of your proposal in the memorandum. Include a statement, stated twice, that motion pictures are an inherently high-risk investment. This may seem counterproductive, but this phrase will protect you from being sued down the line. Anyway, the preponderance of positive news should dwarf these two warnings.

Your memorandum also should spell out how the revenues will be distributed, state the rights and obligations of both the production and the investors and contain a timetable for preproduction through postproduction. Financial protection should be made clear. It is common to put in writing that all funds will be kept in escrow and that monthly financial statements will be provided to all.

Also, be sure to include the following statement (which is the subtle difference between your investment memorandum and a prospectus): *This is not a prospectus but is purely informational in nature.* This will legally allow you to approach more potential investors than otherwise permitted under limited partnership restrictions (see "limited partnership").

Investment memoranda are not for amateurs. It's important that you do not scare away those with deep pockets by presenting an improper agreement, or that you leave loopholes that better-informed investors can drive a Brinks truck through. For these reasons, before drafting any such document, you'll need the expertise of an attorney (if one is your executive producer this will be part of his job) or you will need to study a similar, lawyer-drafted agreement and follow its legalese closely.

Make the entire package look as professional as possible with business cards, printed folders and production company letterhead. Appearance is paramount when you're trying to convince people to invest in what you're selling as a high-quality production.

Finally, here's some ammo to add to your sales pitch. These are only a few of the many statistics available that illustrate (place tongue firmly in cheek) the "truckloads of cash" waiting to be picked up by those who invest in independent cinema. The grosses are estimates (not adjusted for today's dollars), including all worldwide revenue. They grow into perpetuity from video and TV sales, screenings and miscellaneous ancillaries.

	Budget	Gross
Pink Flamingos	$12,000	$10,000,000+
Roger & Me	$140,000	$12,000,000+
The Brothers McMullen	$24,000	$15,000,000+
The Legend of Boggy Creek	$120,000	$27,000,000+
Sling Blade	$1,200,000	$40,000,000+
Benji	$550,000	$65,000,000+
Friday the 13th	$650,000	$80,000,000+
Halloween	$320,000	$90,000,000+
sex, lies, and videotape	$1,200,000	$110,000,000+

For those of you looking to raise multi-millions, the indie-studio film *Pulp Fiction*, budgeted at $7,000,000, has so far made more than $225,000,000.

Sure, all of this paints a somewhat skewed picture. Sure, it stacks the deck in your favor. That's the idea.

CORPORATIONS

Going public, either by creating a **public corporation** or a **subchapter "S" corporation** (the "S" stands for small) will allow you to solicit and receive investments from an unlimited number of people and it will protect them from liability. Unfortunately, it's also a major pain in the posterior.

The worst part about corporations is that your profits can be taxed twice, once at the corporate level and again on your individual tax form (this is minimized somewhat with an "S"-corp, and the business tax can be eliminated by setting up your corporation in the states of Delaware and Nevada). Furthermore, the costs ($750 filing fee in New York City) and complications in starting and running such an enterprise (such as dealing with the Securities and Exchange Commission) usually outweigh the advantages for an indie on a shoestring. However, if your budget is at least in the high six figures and you have the proper legal assistance, incorporating is worth consideration.

Joint ventures (JVs) are common when two or more production companies merge to make a movie. But they can also be used by films to set up separate entities: a producing "S"-corp and a financing "S"-corp. In this way, investors deal only with the financing corporation. They experience limited liability and little or no double taxation. Meanwhile, you can run the production from the producing corp with no interference from your investors. JVs have their own restrictions, which vary from state to state (multiple tax filings are expensive and time-consuming), but they are another option to consider—with legal assistance, of course.

LIMITED LIABILITY COMPANY

Somewhere between a corporation and a limited partnership is a limited liability company (LLC). This combines the liability protection of a corporation with the tax benefits of a limited partnership; as well, it has some of the restrictions of both. Rules vary from state to state, but limited liability companies generally cost less to set up than limited partnerships (often there are no filing fees), but they cost more to run (annual fees in New York City are $650, minimum). In recent years, some indie filmmakers have utilized LLCs with good results. *Spanking the Monkey* (1994; its budget was $200,000) and *Manny and Lo* (1996; $700,000) were both financed this way. Again, consult a lawyer and read the fine print if you plan to set up a limited liability company.

LIMITED PARTNERSHIP

Limited partnerships (LPs) are among the most common methods of independently producing a film which has a budget of less than $2 million. *Welcome to the Dollhouse* (1996; $700,000) and *Jeffrey* (1995; $1.7 million) were both financed with LPs. Again, the laws vary from state to state, but the basic definition remains: A limited partnership is made up of two parties—the **general partner** (usually the producer) and the **limited partners**. The limited partners are silent investors whose liability is restricted to the extent of their capital contribution. (In other words, the people buying into your high-risk dream are protected against such items as budget overruns, unpaid loans and lawsuits.) For this protection, they forfeit any say in the production. Limiting the investors' creative input may be an LP's most appealing feature, or the best part may be that unlike corporations, profits are only taxed once, as personal income.

The main disadvantage to an LP is that while your investors' liability is limited yours is not. If, for example, a grip falls off a ladder, breaks his leg and sues you, you could lose your house. For this reason, with any LP you'll also want to procure comprehensive liability and worker's comprehensive insurance (both are major expenses).

The standard limited partnership agreement provides that net producers' profits are split equally between the general partner and the limited partners, but the general partner (you) will not typically participate in the profits until the total outlay of the investors has been paid. However, if the budget is sufficient, there should be salaries for the producer and director and/or an open expense account. Try to write these up-front dollars into the budget for yourself.

Having said that, do not use an expense account as a slush fund. Sleazy producers have been known to set up LPs by tantalizing investors with Academy Award winners who are "tentatively attached." Once the producer collects the money, he doesn't even try to get the flick going. Instead, he lives high off the slush fund and, predictably, the project eventually falls through. To protect everyone's money and your reputation, don't open such an account until shooting commences, at which time legitimate personal preproduction costs can be deducted retroactively.

A limited partnership agreement should be written by an expert or, at the very least, a similar, completed document should be consulted while yours is being drafted. LPs are usually filed with your county clerk's office. Fees can be costly.

Complications with limited partnerships can arise when it comes to soliciting. Laws restrict both the number of potential investors who may be approached and the number who can participate. In California, the maximum to approach is twenty-five; the maximum to participate is ten. In order to approach more than the maximum, you're suppose to start over again at zero and form a new LP, filing again with the county clerk and again paying all fees.

These are the laws. However, there are a few square miles of gray area here. If you mention to a hundred people that you need some cash for a movie is that considered soliciting? What if a hundred people just happen to hear about it? Or what if your friends tell their friends and their friends tell their rich uncles and . . . ? Don't get paranoid. The odds are against the Securities and

Exchange Commission having spies at your party. The thing to avoid is making a public offering. Don't do something stupid like putting an ad in *The Wall Street Journal*. And remember: Your investment memorandum, "purely informational in nature," is, as far as anyone is concerned, not a prospectus and, therefore, you can technically show it to a thousand folks and then make an "official" pitch to only those who express further interest. This is not a prospectus. This is not a prospectus. This is not . . .

Know the laws in your area for your situation, and know how to dance around them.

FOREIGN FINANCING

Without a proven track record and with no name actors attached, it will be very difficult to attract international money. But if you have some experience (a distributed feature or, at the very least, an award-winning short) and if you have a "name" signed on, foreign funding may be within reach. American indie veterans Jim Jarmusch (*Mystery Train*) and Hal Hartley (*Trust*) sustain their idiosyncratic film careers with European and Japanese money.

Some foreign governments would love to have your business. They offer tax incentives, low or no-interest loans, advances on production costs or even cash subsidies in an effort to foster motion picture production. But, of course, they want something in return. To take advantage of their enticements, you almost always need to shoot on their soil and utilize their technicians, facilities, supplies and actors. Frequently, such a U.S. production is limited in the number of "key elements" (director, actors, producers, cinematographer) it can bring from America—sometimes to a scant total of two! Needless to say, this can be a major roadblock.

The American film *Before Sunrise* (1994) was made in Austria with funding from that government. And the U.S. indie *Cold Fever* (1996) was shot for $1.6 million in Japan and Iceland with local crews; its co-producers were German and Swiss; it had American and German investors; it utilized free Icelandic production services. Wherever you're thinking of going, information on subsidies, requirements, and foreign production companies is available through that nation's film commission. Contact their embassy (in Washington, D.C. or New York City). You'll almost always need to join forces with a production company "over there." Choose one with low-budget experience.

Shooting on foreign soil is a big deal, way beyond the scope of most nonstudio films. A more feasible approach is to find people or companies overseas willing to invest in your project while allowing you to shoot in North America. For example, Germany has government-sponsored regional film funds that support intriguing projects, including U.S. indies; France also has several producers and distributors willing to front money, including UGC (*The Doom Generation*), the prolific CiBy 2000 (*Lost Highway*), and the L.A.-based Lumiere International (*Leaving Las Vegas*). Among the best resources in England is *Channel Four* which has financed edgy flicks worldwide. Japan, Italy and Spain all have numerous film investors. And, of course, financiers can be found anywhere on the globe. Wherever there's wealth, there are people who can potentially be drawn to the "glamour" of American film production.

You can meet in person with various global bankrollers if you're among the lucky few accepted to an overseas investment forum. The International Film Financing Conference (IFFCON) is held each February in San Francisco (sixty indie producers were admitted to the 1997 conference). The documentary *Crumb* (1994) is a successful graduate of this conference. Slightly more prestigious is Cinemart, an annual event held every January in Rotterdam, Holland (it had a mere dozen U.S. invitees in 1997). The newest addition, the IFP's No Borders is staged in conjunction with the Independent Feature Film Market (IFFM) in New York City each September. Each of these forums allows you to pitch your project to international investors and distributors.

The most important factor in obtaining foreign funding will be the **package**: the script, proven production people (especially, the director) and name actors. It will be nearly impossible to get overseas cash (or substantial U.S. financing, for that matter) without "names" attached. Therefore, try to obtain letters from known actors, in which they commit to your project if the money materializes. (Realize that "names" here may be "no-names" in other countries, and vice versa.)

Another factor considered by international investors is whether or not your movie has direct relevance to their country. Many overseas dollars come from pre-sales to theatrical and television distributors. It shouldn't come as a surprise that the typical Italian or German is not all that interested in the angst of minor league baseball players in Milwaukee.

25

Foreign capital is the lifeblood of some indie filmmakers. But for rookies without a name, without significant "stars" attached and with a uniquely American story, it's best not to expend time chasing rainbows in Pakistan; it'll be hard enough finding gold in Peoria.

BANK LOANS

From $100 million studio efforts to $1 million indies, banks can and do provide loans to film productions. As a first-time filmmaker, even you can secure a loan. No matter who you are, the key is, before borrowing a dime, you must have an agreement with a reputable distributor contractually stating it will buy and release your movie when it is completed. This may be either a **distribution guarantee** or a **negative pickup** deal. But, you gotta have it. Banks are not venture capitalists: no distribution agreement, no loan.

Loans are paid out weekly and they're contingent on the film being finished. Therefore, the total amount borrowed will rise if your budget bulges during production. This brings up the major difference between a guarantee and a negative pickup. In a distribution guarantee, the distributor covers budget overruns; in a negative pickup, the distributor does not. Because of this, assuming the distributor is in healthy financial shape, most banks will readily lend money to any motion picture with a distribution guarantee. (Such agreements are used mostly by studios.)

On the other hand, negative pickups are a common method for financing nonstudio features with budgets in the $1 million to $7 million range. *Reservoir Dogs* ($1.5 million) and *The Usual Suspects* ($5.5 million) were both funded this way. In a negative pickup situation, because the distributor does not guarantee the loan, the production is responsible for any budget overruns. Therefore, you'll also need to obtain a **completion bond** which will cover excess expenses totaling up to 100 percent of the original budget. The bond will cost approximately an additional four percent of your total budget and can be obtained from a bonding company.

The ability to get bonded, in turn, will be based primarily on your budget, your shooting schedule, any potential problems (such as an actor with a high-risk history), and the track records of the producer, director and unit production manager (UPM) for bringing pictures in on-budget. Devoid of such a record, you may need to hire a reliable UPM—mandated by the bonding company. Whatever the circumstances, bonders will want to protect themselves and will most probably require you also have a ten percent contingency in your budget.

With either a distribution guarantee or a negative pickup deal, banks want to make sure they'll get their money back. Foreign and video distribution are as good as domestic theatrical distribution in these matters, and creditors like the guaranteed fees of television as opposed to unpredictable box office grosses. The best way to ease a bank's worries is to have a substantial distribution advance (ideally as much as the budget/loan) put into escrow early. In addition to collecting interest on the loan (typically the prime rate plus one percent), the creditor will often participate in the producer's share of profits, so they will be very concerned with your movie's long-term success.

Of course, all of this depends upon your obtaining a distribution guarantee or (more likely) a negative pickup deal, and that's the hard part. Because you need to sell your film before there's a film, any deal depends on the marketing prospects of your movie. Key indicators are the script, your proven abilities as a director (if any), your budget vs. sales estimates, and (most importantly) the name actors committed. Star performers (the kind who bring audiences into theaters) are nearly mandatory for any deal leading to a loan. Hence the term "bankable cast."

Setting up your film with a distributor and/or financial institution will require paperwork, research and expertise. Distribution companies and banks will have requirements about what the finished product looks like (major changes in the cast, script or visual style can void the contract; they're banking on a certain movie). Bonding companies will have regulations about your budget and spending habits. And once an institution takes over financing, their accountants will want continuous itemized expense records from your first check to your last. Furthermore, if the bank has a slice of the profits, it will want reports forever on money earned.

To secure a deal, you'll need an attorney; to keep a deal running smoothly, you'll need an accountant. Do not try to negotiate the Byzantine intricacies of release agreements and bank loans without guidance.

And without a distribution guarantee or negative pickup deal, don't waste time dreaming about loans. No banker will do much more than smile, cash your penny rolls and show you the door.

GRANTS

Look, it's free cash! There are thousands of public and private organizations offering money for the arts. Documentaries specialize in searching for grant financing. But narrative features can also obtain endowments, especially if your story deals with a social issue or features a specific demographic group.

Say you're planning a fictional film to be shot in Minneapolis, featuring a cast and crew of Native Americans and dealing with handgun violence. You could approach local and regional arts foundations, Native American organizations, and gun control public interest groups. Even if such associations don't officially offer grants, don't be bashful about asking. Perhaps they'll initiate such a program at your suggestion and honor you as their first recipient. It's unlikely, but, depending on your project, it's not impossible.

Subject matter is paramount. *Daughters of the Dust*, a poetic tale of African-Americans set in 1902 and based on little-known history, was financed with grants, including research cash from the Guggenheim Endowment and more than $1 million from PBS's *American Playhouse*. *Stand and Deliver*, a 1988 independent feature based on the true story of students in East L.A. studying to take the Advanced Placement Test in calculus, received all of its $1.37 million budget from public and private foundations, including $687,000 from *American Playhouse* and the Corporation for Public Broadcasting; $350,000 from ARCO; $172,000 from the National Science Foundation; and $50,000 from the Ford Foundation. Additionally, Pepsi and Anheuser-Busch chipped in $37,500 and $12,000, respectively, for product placement. The producer spent a year working full-time raising this cash, but it was worth it. *Stand and Deliver* received critical acclaim, Independent Spirit awards, an Academy Award nomination for its star (Edward James Olmos) and it grossed more than $20 million.

For political reasons, the big bucks from PBS are now harder to come by. Still, there are literally thousands of sources for grants. For documentarians, the pursuit of grant money is a major component of their job description. In fact, many doc productions hire **grant writers** to specifically search for and negotiate the endowing of award money. Employing such a person probably is not a wise investment for a narrative film, with the possible exception of a true "social issue" movie.

When you find places that seem appropriate for your movie, ask for their grant guidelines. Regulations are sometimes prohibitive. Needless to say, don't relinquish any creative control. And don't seriously alter your vision for a few thousand dollars (a few hundred thousand dollars may be another story!). Applications vary but grant administrators usually want to see something resembling your investment memorandum package (script, budget, resumés, reels), with the addition of an essay on your objectives and how your movie will better the world for your fellow human beings.

Don't get your hopes up: Narrative films that receive institutional funding are almost always those that have the right message at the right time with the right people behind them. Explore the possibilities, but don't make grant-chasing your primary financing focus.

CREDIT CARDS

Since Robert Townsend partially paid for his 1987 indie hit *Hollywood Shuffle* with a collection of credit cards, this type of "financing" has been considered a viable method for micro-budget filmmaking. But, beware: For every story of credit card success, there are dozens of stories of plastic disaster. Do not stake your future on a mountain of debt. It seems an unnecessary caution, but, because of the emotions involved in art, people often let their hearts overwhelm their brains. Independent filmmaking is a very high-risk venture. Do not send away for ten credit cards and max out their limits unless you and your family are prepared for the worst-case scenario: years of working multiple jobs to pay off the debt while dodging collection agencies and court orders.

If your film is accepted into a major festival but you're broke and you need to get the damn thing finished so quickly that you don't have time to shop for completion funds, you may—after carefully weighing the risks—want to use a credit card or two. But keep your eyes open and your brain clear. Plan for the worst, and never get into more debt than you can safely climb out of.

BY ANY MEANS NECESSARY

Many of you reading this book will be self-financing your film, perhaps with help from family and friends. Probably this will mean that your dream project will be budgeted at less than $200,000 (perhaps much less) and that you'll have to scrape and claw to come up with every cent.

Methods of raising money are limited only by your imagination. The key to getting it done though is not really in the scrounging, whether it be Robert Rodriguez allowing a research center to conduct medical experiments on him in order to forage the funds to make *El Mariachi*, Michael Moore staging bingo games to help finance *Roger & Me*, or Robert Townsend and his *Hollywood Shuffle* credit card collection.

The key is in keeping your costs down. *Clerks* was made for $27,000 because it was shot in the convenience store that employed writer/director Kevin Smith. *The Brothers McMullen* was produced for $24,000 in filmmaker Ed Burns's family house with his mom doing the "catering." *Slacker* was filmed for $23,000 because Richard Linklater picked up scenes whenever he could get his friends behind and in front of the camera.

These films represent the true spirit of "by any means necessary." By keeping the initial production costs to less than $30,000, almost anyone can make a movie. Therefore, much of the remainder of this guide will be dedicated to cost-cutting measures.

Meanwhile, you do whatever it takes to get the money. You have to, because you're a filmmaker, and you have a burning, aching desire to make a certain film. You must make your dream come true. If you don't feel this way, if you don't believe in your vision or your story or yourself, if you don't have that burning, aching desire, then go sell insurance for a couple years: you're not ready to make a movie yet.

PREPRODUCTION

3/SCHEDULE

One of the first things the producer or unit production manager needs to do is set a timetable for the movie, encompassing preproduction through post-production. Every film is unique, therefore, samples should not be taken as prescriptions; however, it may be helpful to review a sample calendar for an independent feature film. Week one begins after the script is approved and money is secured.

TIMETABLE EXAMPLE

Week 1	Prepare budget; begin securing principal crew members (cinematographer, unit production manager, production designer, assistant director, editor)
Weeks 2-3	Scout locations; begin casting
Weeks 4-5	Continue casting; begin set construction; continue securing other crew positions
Week 6	Complete casting; begin rehearsals; secure locations; obtain permits & insurance
Week 7	Continue rehearsals; secure equipment, props, costumes; begin set design
Week 8	Dress rehearsals; meet with crew; continue production design; pick up equipment
Weeks 9-12	PRODUCTION. Editor begins assembling rough cut electronically

Week 13	Editor completes rough cut
Weeks 14-20	Edit picture; compose music
Weeks 21-24	Edit sound; score music
Week 25	Mix sound
Week 26	Cut negative; film transfer process
Week 27	Answer print made

All of these elements will be described in detail throughtout the rest of this book. For now, it's important to know that the sooner you secure key people (such as unit production manager, cinematographer and assistant director), the better off preparation will be. Assemble your team to go through preproduction together.

One of the real advantages of independent filmmaking is that people are often available in preproduction for little or no salary. For example, cinematographers on studio flms often punch in only a couple weeks before production begins because their salaries are so high and their calendars so full. But a less experienced (lower-budget) cinematographer may happily hit the ground running months prior and for free. Similarly, while millionaire movie stars may not do any rehearsals, less-experienced actors may be happy to participate in as many practice runs as you can schedule.

BREAKDOWN & SHOOTING SCHEDULE
The assistant director or production manager (on low-budget films, this may be the same person) will break down the shooting script. In a **continuity breakdown,** the screenplay is divided into numerical scenes or sequences and the following information is noted:

- page length and a brief synopsis of each scene / sequence;

- cast members to appear;

- extras needed;

- the location;

- whether it's a day or a night shoot;

- the need for any special equipment, wardrobe, props, cars, effects, etc.;

- any other notes of significance.

Just like a studio picture, this information can be noted with color-coded strips placed on an official **breakdown board.** If you don't have such tools, you can easily manage without.

The real value of a breakdown becomes apparent when creating a **shooting schedule**. First determine how many days you can shoot. The most important factor in this will be your budget, but your style and shooting strategy will also impact the decision, as will the availability of actors, equipment and locations.

For features costing less than $500,000, eighteen to twenty-four shooting days are the norm. Better-financed indies can go for thirty days or more. The more days the better, of course, but, because of high-priced budget items such as salaries, equipment, location fees, film stock and food, how many days you go is one of your most important financial considerations. Micro-budgeters beware: A shooting schedule of fewer than fifteen days can be brutal if you want to have a respectable number of takes and setups.

Low-budget indies typically shoot for three or four weeks (six days per week). Do not shoot for more than six days continuously unless you're in the final week because this can create morale problems among your crew, losing you more time than you gain.

In order to save on equipment and locations, some very low-budget pictures shoot only on weekends. Beware that this method can create continuity problems (an extended shoot with five out of every seven days off can make it difficult to duplicate visual elements from weekend to weekend). Also, when filming only two days a week over two to three months, it is often difficult to keep people focused and enthusiastic. Still, if your cast and crew is made up of dependable friends and family who need to keep their real jobs, and if you can get equipment and locations for little or no money on the weekends, this method is worth considering. Obviously, two-day shoots will create unique scheduling concerns. Most importantly, try to eliminate changing locations in the middle of any weekend; this can take a large chunk of your precious time.

Your goal is to shoot all scenes at each particular location at the same time, regardless of where these scenes appear in the script, thus minimizing travel. If you need to move from one spot to another during a shooting day the two locations should be nearby in order to avoid dead time. Also, organize your schedule to utilize your highest paid cast members and any expensive rental equipment on the fewest number of days.

By the way, the location and cast constraints of independent filmmaking sometimes make breakdowns and schedules self-evident. If you have two locations and four speaking parts, it won't be tough to break things down and create your shooting schedule.

SHOOTING STRATEGY

As the director of a low-budget film, you <u>must</u> have a precise plan of attack. You won't have the luxury of covering every element from a variety of angles and later sorting through miles of footage in the editing room. The independent film director frequently has to "**edit in camera**," which means you know before shooting how each scene will be cut and you film only those shots that will later be used.

During preproduction, the shooting script will often change as a schedule is created, locations are secured, actors are cast, a crew is hired and equipment is rented. As faces and places become real, plan your coverage accordingly. Above all else, keep your shooting script flexible: it's a blueprint, not a bible.

From the shooting script, you can create **shot lists**, noting the coverage for each camera setup. Try to utilize the minimum number of setups while maximizing the number of shots you can get. Moving equipment, props, etc., and relighting everything for a new set-up can devour valuable hours.

Diagrams of sets and locations are useful for visualizing your shooting strategy and conveying it to the crew. Note where the camera and actors will be for each shot. As always, try to minimize setups.

You may want to create **storyboards** (a visual representation of shots). Drawing talent is a plus but not mandatory. There are computer programs (not inexpensive) such as *Storyboard Artist* which will delineate the scenes for you. Carefully storyboarded sequences, thought out during preproduction, can save significant time on the set. It's especially helpful to sketch out scenes which have a lot of action or complex camera moves.

4/BUDGET

Whether you have $10,000 or $10 million, it is crucial to plan carefully how your money will be spent. Plot out everything you'll need as early as possible, allowing yourself time to shop for bargains. Budget correctly now—or prepare for compromises and catastrophes later.

PREPARATION

Those of you with no experience may want to hire a good unit production manager to prepare your budget and breakdown/ schedule (see also "SCHEDULE"). You can pay someone a flat fee to do this early in preproduction and bring him (or someone else) onboard full-time during the later stages of film prep.

Whoever does the budgeting will need a few tools. **Industry directories** such as the annual *Hollywood Blu-Book* and *LA 411* are invaluable because they list virtually every lab, stage, equipment rental house, agency—almost every service of value to a producer. Some directories are also available on CD-ROM. If you are operating outside of Southern California, you can pick up the good old **yellow pages** from the nearest city (as well as a business-to-business directory). Also, for around $99, you can get ProCD—white and yellow pages on CD for all of the U.S.; and for a little more, Canada is included.

Some of the best sources for budgeting info are your fellow filmmakers and industry professionals. **Recommendations** are paramount when it comes to hiring crew and securing equipment. Such information can save you much time and money. Consult with entertainment producers in your community, ideally those who've made feature films for a budget similar to yours. If no such person exists, any film, video, or audio producer, director or technician may be able to provide you with names, contact numbers and other tips. Don't be afraid to ask anyone. A good UPM has dozens of connections and sources.

You can't prepare a budget without a **telephone** or two or three. Typically, a producer/UPM spends preproduction with a receiver glued to his ear as he barters, begs and beguiles. Call to get quotes on everything. And, never agree to the price on a published equipment rate card. There will be more about this in the "STOCK" and "STUFF" sections, but for now, know that rate cards are to be used only as bookmarks. The **fax machine** has become almost mandatory to film production companies in recent years as much important and useful information will come to you this way. Meanwhile, you will be faxing out completed release forms, casting notices, etc.

A **computer budgeting program**, such as *Budget Master* or *Movie Magic Budgeting*, can be a useful timesaver. These software programs list every item and every category of a budget (you can also add or subtract categories). You fill in the blanks; the computer does the math. It will also output various breakdowns, specifying where your money is being spent. These programs can make budgeting easier, but you can manage without them.

Finally, at least one person on your team will need acute skills at the fine art of haggling. In most big cities there are several establishments to take your business to. Always be on the verge of going to that other place (that you really don't want to deal with) that gave that better quote (that never came). Prices sink fast when folks think you have options. They don't budge if they know you've got nowhere else to turn. Barter hard. Even if you're in Nowheresville you can always threaten to go to Somewhere City.

ARBITRARY SAMPLE BUDGETS

As with the timetable, what follows are not prescriptions. They are sample budgets told in broad terms. Yours should be more detailed. But for those of you who have never seen a film budget, these samples will help you understand the categories and conceptualize how the money is spent. Everything is subject to change, and almost everything probably will.

Our first budget assumes that you have $100,000 and that you'll be shooting in 16mm or Super 16 for three six-day weeks (eighteen shooting days, total).

$100,000 SAMPLE BUDGET

writer / director / producer(s)	profit points
cast	$3,000
TOTAL ABOVE-THE-LINE COSTS:	$3,000
extras	$ 0
unit production manager /	
assistant director	1,500
production designer	1,300
art director / prop master	800
script supervisor	1,200
cinematographer	1,500
1st assistant camera	1,200
2nd assistant camera	900
gaffer	1,200
electrician	900
key grip	1,200
grip (a.)	900
grip (b.)	900
sound mixer	1,400
boom operator	800
makeup & hair	900
still photographer	0
production assistants	0
craft services & meals	8,000
still expenses	400
props	400
production design / sets	1,100
wardrobe expenses	300
makeup expenses	100
electrical expendables	500
camera rental	5,500
lighting / grip package rental	4,500
dolly	2,400
missing & damage	300
film stock	7,000

audio tape stock & expendables	1,200
sound package rental	1,300
truck rental/gas	400
location fees	1,600
insurance & permits	3,000
telephone	300
miscellaneous office expenses	300
lab fees for negative developing	
& video transfer	15,200

TOTAL PRODUCTION COSTS
(including ABOVE-THE-LINE) <u>$73,400</u>

editor	$2,800
nonlinear edit system	5,000
composer	1,000
music rights	0
ADR	800
sound edit	2,600
sound transfers	600
3-stripe sound stock	800
negative cut	3,700
titles	2,300
answer print	7,000

TOTAL POSTPRODUCTION COSTS (for now) <u>$26,600</u>

TOTAL BUDGET <u>$100,000</u>

"Above-the-line" (ATL) costs refer to the monies paid to the the writer(s), director, producer(s) and principal cast members. (These are the people whose salaries so greatly alter the typical studio film budget.) Ironically, in this budget, above-the-line individuals will receive less money up-front than those working below-the-line.

Obviously, the crew salaries are very low. In order to attract quality people for critical roles (such as cinematographer) you may need to move over funds from other categories. From where? Well, virtually anything can conceivably be obtained for nothing or nearly nothing. Sometimes, money can be saved from such line items as makeup artist or boom operator by hiring someone who will work gratis ("gratis" always means screen credit and meals; it usually also means gas money and a video copy of the completed film) or for **deferred pay** (See "Deferrals," to follow).

Another important thing to note is that much more money will need to be spent in post-production. A budget like this will get you a film to shop around for **completion funds** (aka, finishing funds; the financing necessary to finish a 35mm print of your film), but it won't get you a print to screen in a commercial theater. You (or your eventual distributor) will probably need to spend much more for sound editing and mixing, prints, color correcting sessions, music rights, etc. Furthermore, because this budget assumes you're shooting 16mm or Super 16 (see "STOCK: 35, Super 16, 16, Video") you'll need at least an additional $40,000 for a blowup to 35mm film stock. These post-production factors explain why $20,000 movies end up costing ten times that much when they're finally released. *El Mariachi, Clerks, The Brothers McMullen* virtually all so-called micro-budget indies usually required several hundred thousand dollars more than their quoted prices (paid by their distributors) in order to be completed for commercial screens. But, for now, don't worry about that . . . not too much anyway.

In fact, for now, you may not need to worry about any film prints. After editing is complete, you can output a video version from a nonlinear editing system and have something that resembles a completed film. Therefore, you won't need to cut the negative, buy titles, transfer the sound to an optical track or make a 16 or Super 16 answer print—and, you can promptly shave more than $14,000 from this budget . . . for now. Much more about post-production options later. During preproduction, your first concern should be getting the best possible movie "in the can" (shot, but not edited).

For those of you with a few more bucks to spend, what follows is a $1 million budget. It assumes you'll shoot in 35mm (and at more than twice the ratio of the preceding budget) for five weeks at six days a week (thirty shooting days, total).

$1,000,000 SAMPLE BUDGET

writer	$20,000
director	30,000
producer (a.)	30,000
producer (b.)	30,000
cast	180,000
payroll taxes, health & pension	20,000
travel, living & miscellaneous expenses	6,000

TOTAL ABOVE-THE-LINE COSTS $316,000

extras	$4,000
casting director	$11,000
casting assistant	3,000
casting expenses	2,000
unit production manager	12,000
production supervisor	4,500
secretary	2,000
location manager	4,000
1st assistant director	7,500
2nd assistant director (a.)	3,600
2nd assistant director (b.)	3,600
production designer	6,000
art director	3,600
prop master	2,400
script supervisor	5,500
cinematographer	12,000
1st assistant camera	5,500
2nd assistant camera	4,500
2nd unit camera operator	3,600
gaffer	6,000
best boy electric	4,500
electrician	3,600
key grip/dolly grip	6,000
grip (a.)	3,600
grip (b.)	3,600
grip (c.)	3,600
sound mixer	6,000
boom operator	3,600

costume designer	4,500
wardrobe assistant	2,000
makeup	4,500
makeup assistant	2,000
hair stylist	4,500
still photographer	4,000
production assistants (7) (expenses)	1,400
payroll taxes	10,000
craft services & meals	22,000
still expenses	1,600
props	3,200
production design & set construction	14,000
wardrobe expenses	3,000
makeup & hair expenses	1,000
electrical expendables	2,200
camera package rental	18,000
2nd unit camera package	6,000
lighting/grip package	14,000
dolly	7,000
missing & damage	1,600
film stock	30,000
audio tape stock & expendables	4,200
sound package rental	6,000
truck(s)/gas/driver(s)	3,000
generator(s)	6,000
location fees	13,000
location cleaning & damage	1,500
insurance	30,000
permits	6,000
police & fire	4,000
legal fees	10,000
telephones	1,000
miscellaneous office expenses	1,200
lab fees for negative develop & video transfer	50,000

TOTAL PRODUCTION COSTS
(including ABOVE-THE-LINE) $749,200

editor	12,000
assistant editor	3,600

nonlinear edit system	8,000
composer	7,500
musicians	6,000
recording facility	4,500
musical expenses	2,000
music rights	50,000
ADR	4,500
actors' ADR allowance	2,000
sound editor(s) & expenses	12,500
sound mixer(s) & expenses	8,000
sound transfers	2,000
3 stripe sound stock	1,600
negative cut	5,000
titles	8,000
opticals	5,000
telecine	16,000
answer print	12,000
miscellaneous lab expenses	1,600
publicity expenses	5,000

TOTAL POSTPRODUCTION COSTS $176,800

SUBTOTAL $926,000

contingency of 8% $74,000

TOTAL BUDGET $1,000,000

Most significant in this budget are the cast and crew salaries: they are now receiving respectable money, allowing you to attract proven talent more easily.

At this level, many items tend to settle and increase only slightly (or not at all) as $1 million grows to $2 million or $3 million. After all, if you're shooting at the same ratio, film stock and lab fees shouldn't be anymore expensive even if a movie costs one hundred million. What does change dramatically are above-the-line salaries (particularly for name actors) and items such as travel and living expenses, stunts, opticals and a full orchestral score. Also, bigger budgets will likely have a bank loan requiring interest, a completion bond and a ten percent contingency. If you include such other items as insurance, legal fees, accounting and SAG bonds (see "CAST:

SAG") more than one-third of your movie's money can be wrapped up in these "paper" categories.

DEFERRALS

Deferrals are arrangements for paying later. Sometimes, as in the case of equipment rental or lab fees, specific dates for payment are agreed to. Most of the time, however, it is stated that the person is paid *if and when your production makes money*. If your film doesn't show a profit (the vast majority of festival-bound indies don't come close), then those who dreamed of receiving deferred pay won't see a dime.

Deferrals are common in low-budget filmmaking, but be advised to utilize them only as a last resort (last resorts are also common in low-budget filmmaking) and only with people who you are confident will show up every day. For non-friends and non-family, spell out clearly the terms for deferrals in a written contract. State a specific sum (not profit points) to be paid if and when you make back all your money and turn a ten percent profit. The truth is deferrals are too often a polite way of ripping off nice people. As a general policy, do not use deferrals . . . unless you have to.

5/PAPERWORK

Policies, permits and releases may start to pile up in the final days of preproduction. The producer should keep all of this paperwork filed in a safe place. Some time in the future, one of these seemingly insignificant forms may be crucial to the lawyers at a video company or television network that wants to distribute your film. Keep essential documents *forever*—or until a distributor or insurance company takes them off your hands (in which case, keep photocopies of them *forever*).

INSURANCE

Film production policies are made up of the following categories:

- **Property damage liability** (P.D.L.) pays for damage to items rented by the production. It excludes vehicles, camera and sound equipment, lighting and grip gear, props, sets and wardrobe (all of which are covered under other insurance categories). You need P.DL. when renting most any stage or location.

- **Comprehensive liability** protects the production against claims of bodily injury or property damage while filming on public land; it also includes all rented vehicles. You'll need this coverage in order to acquire most permits.

- **Miscellaneous equipment coverage** insures owned or rented camera packages, sound, lighting and grip equipment. It can be expanded to include other gear. Without this insurance, you probably will not be able to rent this expensive and fragile equipment.

- **Props, sets and wardrobe coverage** insures (you guessed it!) props, sets and wardrobe. This may be an item your production can do without.

- **Negative film and videotape insurance** protects you against physical loss of raw or exposed film and tape stock. It *excludes* fogging, faulty equipment or developing mishaps, all of which are covered by **faulty stock, camera & processing insurance**. Those of you with very low budgets may wish to skip these categories and hope for the best. Generally, respected labs reimburse costs if they make an error processing your film.

- **Errors and omissions** (E & O) **insurance** covers the production company against lawsuits for issues such as unauthorized use, plagiarism, defamation of character, invasion of privacy, etc. E & O will be mandated by any distributor before releasing your film; they usually pay for it. However, before they can acquire E & O, you'll need to get signed releases for virtually every identifiable person, place or thing seen or heard on-screen. In addition, you'll need a "chain of title" demonstrating that you hold the rights to the screenplay.

- **Worker's compensation insurance** provides medical, disability and death benefits for any employees injured or killed while working on your film. In most states, employers are *required* to carry this insurance. Film production companies are considered high-risk and must be insured at a high rate. In order to save money, some small production companies call themselves film distributors (low risk). Furthermore, many producers working with less than $200,000 conveniently forget this category entirely. Be warned, however, that film sets are considered high-risk for a reason. With ladders and lights and heavy equipment there is much potential for trauma on a set. Without adequate workers comp you could personally be held legally responsible for injuries.

- **Cast insurance** reimburses the film production for any expenses incurred if you or one of your actors become sick, injured or dies. All major productions have this coverage, but your's is not a major production. This is an item you might be able to do without. On the other hand, if you have a star in a lead role and/or if you have a bank loan or major investors, cast insurance most likely will be mandatory. Physical exams of all covered parties (at your expense) will be required in order to secure this coverage. If your star has a known drug history, premiums can be outrageously expensive.

Typically, these categories are bundled into one policy with a premium that is approximately two percent of your film's total budget. When puchasing insurance, it's best to go with an agency that has experience in entertainment indemnity. Such firms are located primarily in Los Angeles and New York City, but they'll insure you wherever you are.

So, what kind of coverage do you need? Remember, you're taking a huge risk by making this independent film. Those of you with very slim budgets will probably need to gamble on some items. However, if you have a $2 million budget, spending $40,000 for insurance is a sound investment.

Be sure to get the minimum protection you need to secure permits, equipment and locations. For most of you, this will mean comprehensive liability, property damage liability and miscellaneous equipment. (If you're a true guerilla production, this may mean zero coverage.) After that, if you can afford it, increase coverage and reduce deductibles or add insurance for other categories.

Do what's right for you. You may think of yourself as a struggling artist with a dream, clawing for every scrap of 16mm stock. But if you step back a little, you'll see that you're also the CEO of a production company, employing a lot of people for long hours in an accident-prone environment. If you have the money, protect yourself.

By the way, sometimes the opportunity presents itself for you to acquire "insurance" under the policy of a larger production, paying the fee directly to them. The cost is less than having your own policy, but it still is not cheap. Warning: This is usually a scam, of sorts. It is often a ploy that offers the *illusion* of insurance, thus allowing you to secure permits and rental agreements, but it is usually not adequate coverage. The significant risk probably outweighs any savings.

PERMITS

Film permits are available at the film commission office, county clerk office or city hall nearest where you're shooting. The permit people are there (supposedly) to help you in their quest to drum up community business. Indeed, they may have a library full of location photos; they may assist you in scouting locations; they may even have information on government space you can lease for little or no money. But mostly what they do is exchange your hard-earned or hard-borrowed cash for "permission slips" that are required to film on all public property: sidewalks, streets, parks, beaches . . . .

Permit prices vary. Some communities desperate to attract outside entertainment dollars may not charge you a cent; some high-priced areas of Los Angeles will charge you $1,000 per day. One hundred dollars per day is typical. In towns with little or no film experience, you might be required to get an ordinary business license (since a film permit may be an unknown commodity). There may be filing fees in addition to the permit costs.

Prepare for red tape and lots of questions. Permit offices will generally want to know such things as how many cars you'll be parking; the number of people working; if you'll be using a generator; and whether you'll be doing stunts or other dangerous deeds. When you file for a permit, you have, in effect, put up a flag for the "film cops." Once they know about you and your movie, you may be required to abide by a huge amount of regulations.

First, they'll probably require lots of insurance (including a huge comprehensive liability policy). Additionally, you will probably need to keep a police officer and, under some circumstances, a firefighter on your set at all times (and you'll have to pay their overtime salaries—sometimes more than $75 per hour!).

Of course, you can opt to pass on obtaining permits altogether. Micro-budget films are frequently shot guerilla style. However, be aware of the risks involved. If you get caught, you will certainly be required to obtain a permit, and this can be a major scheduling calamity as commission offices often require a few days to process the paperwork. Additionally, there will probably be a stiff fine to pay. Guerillas must utilize extreme caution.

RELEASES

Releases give you the right to utilize that which doesn't belong to you. Treat release forms as your friends and companions. You'll need releases for all people who appear on camera (except in crowd scenes or fleetingly in the background) and for everyone whose voice is heard. You'll need releases when you film recognizable locations. You'll need releases to use or show copyrighted material (which is almost everything). You'll need releases for songs. You'll need releases. You'll need releases! You'll need releases!

Without these permission slips, you—and later your distributor—could be held liable in a lawsuit. For this reason, errors and omissions insurance will not be issued without the necessary signed release forms, nor will distributors pick up your film without E & O insurance.

So, you'll need releases. Get to work early collecting signatures on these forms.

To give you a sense of the legalese, a sample personal release and a sample property release follow.

Actor's Release:

AUTHORIZATION
TO REPRODUCE PHYSICAL LIKENESS

I hereby expressly grant to said and its employees, agents, and assigns, the right to photograph me and use my picture and other reproductions of my physical likeness (as the same may appear in any still camera photograph and/or motion picture film), in and in connection with the exhibition, theatrically, on television, or otherwise, of any motion pictures in which the same may be used or incorporated, and also in the advertising, exploiting, and/or publicizing of any such motion picture. I further give said company the right to reproduce in any manner whatsoever any recordings made by said company of my voice and all instrumental, musical, or other sound effects produced by me.

I hereby certify and represent that I have read the foregoing and fully understand the meaning and intent thereof, and intending to be legally bound, I do hereby sign this _____ day of _____, ____.

_____

Witness: _____

Property Release:

AUTHORIZATION TO UTILIZE PROPERTY

On this date, _____, ____, permission is hereby granted to _____ (hereinafter referred to as "Producer") to use the property and adjacent area, located at_____ for the purpose of photographing and recording scenes (interior or exterior) for motion pictures, with the right to exhibit and license others to exhibit all or any part of said scenes in motion pictures throughout the world.

Said permission shall include the right to bring personnel and equipment (including props and temporary sets) onto said premises, and to remove the same therefrom after completion of work. The Producer agrees that said property will be in equal condition upon leaving as upon arriving, ordinary wear and tear in accordance with this agreement excepted.

The above permission is granted for _____ days, as may be necessary, for the sum of _____ per day of principal photography in which the said location is used, commencing on or about _____ (subject to change in case of changes in the schedule or weather conditions), and continuing until completion of all scenes and work required. No charge is to be made except for days on which the aforesaid property is actually used for principal photography.

Producer hereby agrees to hold the undersigned harmless of and from any and all liability and loss which the undersigned may incur by reason of any accidents or other damages caused by any of the Producer's employees or equipment on or about the said premises.

The undersigned does hereby warrant and represent to have full right and authority to enter into this agreement concerning the above-described premises, and that the consent or permission of no other person, firm, or corporation is necessary in order to enable Producer to enjoy full rights to the use of said premises, and that the undersigned does hereby indemnify and agree to hold Producer free and harmless from and against any and all loss, liability, or claims of any nature, including, but not limited to attorney's fees, arising from or concerning a breach of the above warranty.

Lessee: _____

_____

Signed: _____

6/SPACE

When directing a film, you've always gotta be somewhere. When it's not your own property and when you're moving in thousands of pounds of equipment and dozens of people, being somewhere can get expensive. As with all production matters, plan now to save later.

LOCATIONS
Generally, it is cheapest to shoot on location; often, it's so cheap, it's free. Indie director Jean-Luc Godard is credited with inventing the guerilla shoot with his film *Breathless* (1959), by notoriously stealing a tracking shot (he hid the cameraman in a wheelbarrow that was, unbeknownst to passersby, pushed down a busy Paris boulevard). However, shooting without permission has been going on since the invention of the motion picture camera.

And, you don't have to "steal" anything to shoot for free. Films can be lensed in your own home (*The Brothers McMullen*) or place of work (*Clerks*) or in deserted or secluded areas (*Return of the Secaucus 7*). You can shoot virtually anywhere for free—if there is no chance of bothering anyone or of attracting the attention of permit-pursuing cops.

If you're shooting for an extended period (a full day or more) on someone else's property, you'll need to have the owner's permission; you may also need to pay a location fee. (Fees tend to decrease in direct proportion to how far away you get from New York City or Los Angeles. The novelty of shooting a movie is greater in small-town middle America.) In many communities, the thrill of having a "major" motion picture lensed may be enough to open free doors to schools, churches, businesses and government buildings.

Doors open easiest when there's a little something extra to grease the hinges, so to speak. For example, as part of a program to teach filmmaking, employ kids from the local school's drama club as interns (aka free p.a.'s). Also, always offer screen credits to thank those who let you use their property (or who do anything for you for free or at a discount). Sometimes, schools and churches would prefer not to be mentioned, especially if your film is, in any way, inappropriate in theme or action. But most folks love the idea of being immortalized in small print on the big screen.

If you can afford it, hire an experienced **location manager** to scout sites and handle all permits and related paperwork. He'll do your initial research by taking photos and measurements and by shooting videotape of the sites.

If you can't afford a location manager, look for a film student or other experience-seeking rookie to work for gas money and a **location scout** credit. Without a manager or scout, this position usually is absorbed by the producer, director and cinematographer.

When scouting, take a tape measure, light meter and video and/or still camera. Keep your eyes and ears open. As always when shopping for property, don't commit until you've checked out everything and thought clearly about the pluses and minuses. While scouting, do the following:

- Check for excess traffic nearby (on land and in the air), mechanical noise or other unwanted sounds, including creaking floors (even the smallest squeak can seem like a scream when pushing a dolly around a quiet set).

- Make note of available lighting. (Fluorescents can cause special problems and will probably have to be replaced or go unused.)

- Watch out for low ceilings, narrow doors and hallways, stairs without elevators and sharp turns in tiny stairways because you'll need adequate overhead space to set up lights and enough access to move in heavy equipment.

- Check for a hard level floor for dolly equipment. No carpet; no linoleum with ingrained patterns or deep cracks; no sagging foundations. Alternative flooring such as plywood sheets can be laid down, as can dolly tracks, but these options take time and money.

- Find out if the property can be made available, in similar condition, at a later date (as in, weeks later). This is important in case you need to return for pickup shots (see "SAVING A MOVIE: Pickups").

- Check for the availability of phones and rest rooms; space for eating; parking; and a convenient area for an equipment truck or a secure room for storing gear.

- Try to find sites that are within a forty-five-minute drive of your cast and crew. Also, locations should be similarly close to each other.

Film productions require a lot of electricity. For this reason, most films rely on **generators** (see "STUFF: Truck & Generator"). Under the right circumstances, you can **tie-in** to your location's power source, but this should be done only by an electrical contractor or an experienced technician (perhaps a gaffer). The process is potentially deadly. Be safe rather than sorry. By the way, tying-in on the sly is a huge risk. If you're caught, you'll probably get bounced, if not busted.

When your production leaves a location, do not leave a mess behind! Make sure your cast and crew members treat each location with respect, and make sure everyone cleans up after himself. There's probably a clause in your property release stating that the location be left in the same condition as before production (minus normal wear and tear). Be sure this is adhered to.

Perhaps you're a real guerilla, stealing all your shots on the run and being careful not to use identifiable signs, property or people in unfavorable ways. But if you're not, you'll need **location releases** (see "PAPERWORK: Releases"). In addition to setting the terms for liability, this release form should explain any fees. Get this release form signed as soon as possible! You don't want a property owner to be scared away when your crew shows up with a few tons of equipment. With measly money involved, this happens all too frequently.

Finally, there may be times when you'll need to procure lodging for the cast and crew. It is possible, even on a very limited budget, to shoot your whole movie as a "sleep-over." As an example, for *Return of the Secaucus 7* (budget: $60,000), John Sayles rented an out-of-season ski lodge which served as both the set and lodging for the entire crew.

Sometimes sleep-overs can bond everyone as a team, thus increasing focus and productivity by decreasing outside influences. But this plan can backfire if you house your crew in a cheap or dingy place. Living out of a suitcase is not always a vacation; a few weeks in a dive can seem like a jail sentence and this can lead to morale problems, including possible desertions. Weigh all factors carefully before packing for an extended production stay.

STAGES

Your typical **sound stage** has many advantages: high ceilings, soundproofing, prerigging, scaffolding, cables, appropriate electrical power, wild walls, a smooth floor, convenient parking. And it usually comes with several sweet extras: office space, makeup and dressing rooms (often with showers), rest rooms, kitchen, silent air-conditioning. Modern sound stages are a pleasure to film in . . . but they'll cost you. In fact, their typically high price tags keep them out of reach of many independent filmmakers. But you never know. If you have the right connection or if a facility is just opening or is experiencing a downtime, stage doors can open.

Schools, from junior highs to universities, often have stages, although they likely fall short of state-of-the-art. The best of these will have all the standard advantages of a studio sound stage. But even the worst should have high ceilings, overhead rigging and some wild walls. When classes aren't in session, you may be able to rent or use a school's stage. Sometimes, this can be arranged through the school's drama department to expose students to filmmaking (free p.a.'s).

And remember, all the world's a stage—or at least some of it is. You can easily rent vacant **warehouse space**. Use the location checklist to make sure it's appropriate for you. By the way, you can sometimes work a warehouse setting into your script. *Reservoir Dogs* does this. In fact, Tarantino originally planned to shoot his debut film for $30,000) in 16mm black-and-white and *all* of it was set in a warehouse. The picture eventually was made for $1.5 million, but most of the action still occurs in the same cheap space. Settings such as garages, dance studios and gymnasiums, when written into a screenplay, can also serve as their own pseudo-stages.

Most of you who rent stages will need to build at least one set. Of course, before renting a stage or space, you'll be certain you can construct what you need within its confines and within your budget. Wild walls, lumber and skilled carpenters, to name three components of set design, are not cheap. You can do it yourself, but this can be as taxing as building a small house, both in expense and workload. And, you better know what you're doing. Bad construction looks laughable.

In conclusion, if you opt to shoot on a stage, make sure it's as cheap, realistic and easy to work in as a location. For low-budget films, stages often fail on all three counts.

OFFICES

Low-budget indies sometimes get by without an official office (other than the producer's apartment), but if you can spare the money, you'll benefit from having a professional command center. Because it is perceived as unprofessional, you should never cast a movie from your apartment, so having an office may also save you from renting a casting stage. Any space will do. Drag in some inexpensive furniture, pin a preproduction calendar to the wall, hook up a few phones and a fax machine and go to work. You may even want to make this your editing "suite." Allow money for phone bills and miscellaneous office expenses (these can add up). Additionally, look for or set up a production office near where you'll be shooting.

Trailers are as common around Hollywood shoots as bottled water. The producer gets a trailer; the director gets a trailer; the principal actors all get their own trailers. But, even in the best of circumstances, you'll have a fraction of the budget of most Hollywood movies. So, unless someone lets you borrow his Winnebago, forget about mobile offices.

7/CAST

In directing the actors, the most important thing is to choose the right people. The work, the most important work, is done before the shooting starts, because once you tune the actors with what you want, the direction is no mystery at all—it just works somehow.

— *Milos Forman*

Casting is selecting the people who will bring your dream to life. Arguably, casting is not only the most important component of directing but, after the script, it is the most important element in all of filmmaking. No matter how great the other elements are, if the acting is subpar or if there's a feeling that an actor is wrong for a particular role, your film will be haunted forever. On the other hand, good casting will give your movie a certain symmetry, a feeling of realism and rightness that can smooth glitches and enable a motion picture to soar off the screen.

CASTING DIRECTORS
Producers with budgets greater than $300,000 should invest in a **casting director (c.d.)**. For those of you with lower budgets, sometimes a casting director will take on the right independent film for little or no salary; the odds of this are greatest with a casting director who is just getting into features and hungry for screen credits. Alternatively, if you can talk a good game and if you have a great script, you might be able to convince an established casting director to lend his services for a few days, sort of like pro bono work.

A casting director is an extension of your vision. His job is to bring to your attention the kind of performers *you* want, not the kind he wants. Ideally, these two things are the same, but you need to communicate exactly what it is you're looking for. Be certain you and your c.d. are on the same wavelength in regards to physical type and acting ability.

Casting directors are scouts; they evaluate talent. Ideally, your c.d. will have established connections in the independent film scene. He should know plenty of Screen Actors Guild (SAG) actors willing to work for guild minimum salaries and/or non-SAG theatrical actors. And he should certainly be able to find many more.

The casting director may do the initial screening and even the initial auditions without you. It is common for the c.d. to videotape the first call. You can then watch the videos and select which actors to call back. At **callbacks** (additional auditions) actors usually read for the director, producer and any executives—with or without the casting director present. You (the director and the producer) have final say about which performers are hired.

TROLLING FOR TALENT

Without a casting director, you'll have to throw the first net. One common method of casting for a production—big or small, with or without a c.d.—is to list the project with **Breakdown Services Ltd.** They have offices in Los Angeles, New York City, and Vancouver, Canada. Breakdown Services reads and synopsizes your script, writes character descriptions, collects other pertinent information (actors' pay, shooting dates, etc.) and disburses the information to talent agencies. The cost to you is zero (agencies pay Breakdown Services). If an agent's client meets your requirements, the agent will send the actor's photo and résumé your way. This method reaches many talented people (including SAG actors willing to work for non-SAG wages), letting them know up-front exactly what they're getting into. By the way, Breakdown Services can also assist you in finding a casting director.

Another method for attracting talent is to list your production in the acting trade papers; there is no charge for placing a notice. In Los Angeles, the trades are *Drama-Logue* and *Back Stage West*; in New York, it's *Back Stage*. Briefly describe your movie and be as specific as possible regarding the roles (character traits, age range, physical type, etc.). Also note the start date and length of the shoot, specify whether it's a union or nonunion production and whether there is pay. (Productions without pay usually say, "Copy, credit and meals provided." **Copy** means a video version of the completed film; **credit** means screen credit; **meals** means hot food every six hours.) Request photos and resumés. (WARNING: Rent a mailbox that can handle a deluge. With a single listing in an acting trade paper, you may receive thousands of 8x10s.)

Outside of Los Angeles or New York City, there are **regional casting publications**. Sometimes these focus more on theatrical and commercial roles, but they still should accept ads from film productions. The advice above applies. If a listing is free, cram as much information as you can into it.

You also can put a notice in the classified section of almost **any newspaper**—for a fee, of course. Weekly alternative or arts papers may bring the best response for the least amount of money. Try to put a notice in the "Casting" or "Entertainment Work" section; if this not an option, list your movie in the "Help Wanted" section under the heading: "Actors Wanted."

Another way to get the word out is by posting **notices** at drama schools, arts centers, community theaters—any place where actors congregate. In communities with a large population of artists, your flier can generate responses when placed on almost any bulletin board.

Recommendations carry a lot of weight. Ask around: ask fellow filmmakers for suggestions about skilled performers; ask actors to recommend talented friends or acquaintances; ask casting directors for actors they can suggest (even if these c.d.s aren't working for your production, they may have a few minutes to spare). Contact local **acting teachers** for suggestions on promising students. Coaches are usually honest appraisers.

You can also call **talent agents and managers** directly. Explain your project and needs; inquire as to whether they have appropriate clients willing to work for what you're willing to pay. Of course, they won't be objective observers. And, because money is the principal concern for most agents (who take ten percent of what their clients make) and managers (whose percentage is usually even higher), they may not be anxious to submit their clients for jobs that pay SAG minimum or less. Still, a good agent will want to get under-exposed clients working, especially in feature films. (The long-term rewards of boosting a client's career are potentially great, even if the short-term reward is minimal.)

When you're casting, one of the potential windfalls is free tickets to **plays, screenings and readings**. Tell the event's producers or a performer's agent that you're in the process of casting a feature and request that they arrange "comp" (complimentary) tickets for you. During the performance, evaluate the actors. After the show, you can approach those who captured your interest.

Perhaps the best way to scout talent is to watch **feature films, student films and shorts**, especially those that were cast in your community. It's a great advantage seeing how someone looks and acts *on film*, since that's what you'll be making. Don't be too influenced by the fact that someone else was obviously sold on an actor enough to cast him. Evaluate for yourself. If an actor catches your eye, contact the producer (locate him through the distributor or production company). He should be able to tell you if the actor was easy to work with and will probably know how to reach the person. (SAG can also help you contact actors in the guild.)

Finally, **word of mouth** will bring in many more potential performers. Casting news travels fast through acting communities. An actress submitting for a part may tell her friends. And they'll tell their friends. And they'll tell . . .

Now, back to that deluge of 8x10s you were warned to expect. Let's say you're swimming in a few hundred phone numbers, resumés and 8x10s for each role. Before auditions begin, you'll need to sort through the responses. Concentrate on the **photos** first. Eliminate those who are obviously inappropriate. Garbage dumpsters may soon be overflowing. When some people see a casting notice they figure maybe sometime somebody'll need them so they'd better send off an 8x10 just in case. You might get baby photos for car salesmen or grandmothers for gangsta rappers. Weed out those that just don't cut it. Narrow your focus to the most appropriate forty or fewer for each role.

Next, turn the photos over to the **résumés**, which will be stapled or glued to the back. Be aware of the "Essential Truth of Casting:" struggling actors frequently lie. Therefore, resumés may tell you a lot or they may not tell you a thing. Here's how to read an actor's résumé:

- If you need an actor who will carry your movie and this particular actor's credits are paltry, you should move on. There are times when actors, with no prior acting experience, successfully perform as leads in "naturalistic" films (such as the "real kids" in *Kids*). But, in most cases, you won't have time to train your principal actor.

- Impressive college degrees (especially graduate degrees) can be a plus when casting for intellectual roles because intelligence is tough to fake.

- A plethora of acting classes over several years can at least be a sign that this person is willing to work hard at his craft. Specific training in "acting for the camera" is a plus.

- Experience in music videos, commercials, interviews, news and public access television tells you almost nothing about that person's film acting ability. The only thing it does convey, if there are many such credits, is that this person should be comfortable in front of a camera. Similarly, dancing or singing experience doesn't matter unless you're making a musical. Acting for television, fictional interactive media and film (whether it is a student, short or full-length project) matters most.

- Performers with only stage experience can have problems performing in front of the camera. Stage-trained actors tend to overemphasize their lines and movements so as to be seen and heard by people sitting in the last row of the theater. Unless they alter their tone, the camera will magnify their every line and gesture to an extreme.

- For each credit listed on the résumé, there may be a note about the type of role performed. This facet of resumé writing has a clever, almost standardized language all its own which defines terms very broadly. Here's a translation of what some of the key words may mean:

  (1) "Featured" usually means *extra*.

  (2) "Starring," "lead" or "principal" means *a few lines or more*. (It should have been a major role, but it could have

only been a single scene. Unfortunately, there's no way of telling from these words.)

(3) A specific character name with no other information can mean either *extra* or *a few lines or more*. (It could have been a major role; it could have been background filler with a name. Don't assume anything.)

(4) Listings in known projects without an explanation probably mean *extra*. It could even mean the character ended up on the cutting room floor.

- Be aware that height, weight and (especially) age are frequently incorrect. Sometimes they are not even close.

- Any actor with several lines in several SAG films, network television shows and/or national commercials should be a member of SAG. If he has a wealth of impressive credits but he's not in the guild, you'll know such roles were insignificant or he's exaggerating heavily on his resumé.

Some actors may note the availability of a **reel** (video clips of acting performances) or they may send one to you automatically. Reels are a good way of checking on the actor's listed credits and they're great for seeing how someone looks and sounds on film/video. When watching, try to concentrate on how an actor communicates with his fellow performers and the audience (camera). A reel can't tell you if an actor is absolutely right for a role but it can eliminate those who are positively wrong.

AUDITIONS

Short of hiring a known performer of known abilities, auditions matter most. If an actor can nail a role at an audition with all the pressure on, then he should be even better after rehearsing the part. But beware: this is not always true. After experiencing several hundred **cold readings** (auditions in which the actor does not study the part beforehand), some become expert auditioners, not actors. Still, auditions are the best system yet created for discerning the talented.

To prepare for the auditions, pull **sides** (scenes or parts of scenes) for each character. It's important that you attempt to see the actor's full range of emotions required for the role. If he has to cry, crack jokes or scream in pain, excerpt segments of the screenplay that showcase these emotions. Keep the total amount of audition material to less than six pages.

As was mentioned, if you have a casting director, he'll probably do the initial call, but let's proceed as though you're casting on your own. Set up a comfortable place (office, conference room, stage), and start scheduling actors; a contact number should appear on their resumés. Make the sides available (via fax, if possible) upon phoning so that, at their own initiative, they can study the part in advance.

Schedule auditions every fifteen to thirty minutes and, if possible, group together all applicants for a specific character. (It's usually easier to make judgments if you read everyone for Character A before moving on to Character B.)

Appearances come first. Be certain an actor—in person—looks the part; people often appear different from their 8x10s. Voices can surprise you, as well. Trust your eyes and ears—not a photo and definitely not an age, weight or height statistic. If you want someone to change his hair or wear special makeup, tell him at the first meeting. If he won't do it, move on.

From the beginning, note if a person is prompt, courteous and easy to work with. If he has an attitude when he's at what is essentially a job interview, it'll only get worse when he has the job and things don't go his way (i.e., the food is too cold or the set is too hot or the day is too long.) After all, not everyone will be thrilled to slave away on your quirky little movie; many would rather be doing a sitcom pilot or shampoo commercial.

Have someone other than yourself feed lines (read the other roles). At this point, memorization is not important. Notice how the actor gives and takes with his counterpart; is he listening or is he simply reading? Good acting is all about *re*acting and *inter*acting. Watch for "real" emotions behind the words.

During an audition, some performers read lines flat, like reciting an IRS form (especially if they're nervous); or, they overexaggerate emotions, attempting to impress you with their depth of feeling. Obviously, neither reading is correct. Lines must sound and feel real and contain the proper amount of passion and resonance. If you know your script and if you have an overall vision of your film, you'll know when someone gets it right.

Make sure that prospective actors can do everything they'll need to do, not only in their range of acting ability but also with regard to any special skills required. If the role requires singing or fighting or roller skating—ask them do do it during the audition. Usually, there is little time for on-the-job training; if an actor can't pull it off during the audition, assume he won't be able to do it with cameras rolling.

It's crucial that a performer be able to take direction from you. Even if he's reading something perfectly, ask him to do it another way, and then another, especially if it's a particularly stressful role. If he doesn't respond well to your prodding, it's better to find out now. By the way, if an actor wants to try anything over again, let him. Those who ask for another take often nail it the next time.

Be polite to everyone who auditions. Don't dismiss anyone too early. Auditioning can be emotionally grueling for the actors. Recognize the awesome power you hold when you judge someone's occupational talent and physical appearance. Wield this power with a velvety palm. If an actor is good, it's okay to compliment him, but don't commit a role to anyone during the audition. Wait until you've seen all prospective actors and have had time to contemplate each of them individually, as well as the cast as a whole.

Narrow the field to six or fewer people for each role. Bring them in for a callback. At this point, make the completed script (or a significant portion of it) available. This will allow actors to gain a greater familiarity with the story and characters. And it will enable you to evaluate them under conditions closer to actual acting and not just under the process of auditioning.

Somewhere along the way, it's helpful to find out how each auditioning actor responds to a (video) camera. Some people perform differently and/or look or sound different on film or tape. Beware of camera shyness (common among beginners) or of artificial "performing" (common among those with only theatrical experience).

Again, narrow the field. Schedule as many callbacks as necessary. Someone for each role should step forward to make it his own. If this doesn't happen, start over again, bringing in new faces. Value believability, compatibility, intelligence, presence and genuine emotion.

RECOGNIZABLE NAMES

More and more familiar faces are popping up in independent films. Performers such as Steve Buscemi, Lili Taylor and Tim Roth seem ubiquitous to off-Hollywood cinema in the 1990s. Even superstars (past and present) Robert Mitchum and Johnny Depp starred in *Dead Man* (1995), a black-and-white "art western." *Dead Man* was directed by indie veteran Jim Jarmusch, but a filmmaker's inexperience is not necessarily a liability in securing "names" for independent productions. Then-tyro Quentin Tarantino (his resumé highlight: video store clerk) and then-unknown Bryan Singer both secured casts brimming with recognizable faces for, respectively, *Reservoir Dogs* and *The Usual Suspects* (1995). Neophyte John Dahl was able to cast Nicholas Cage, Dennis Hopper and Lara Flynn Boyle in *Red Rock West* (1993). Even George Huang (resumé highlight: studio errand boy), with a $250,000 budget, managed to get Kevin Spacey to headline his film, *Swimming with Sharks* (1994). The list goes on.

Why do name actors perform in low-budget flicks by no-name directors? Sometimes financially successful stars feel legitimized by appearing in such a film after having made their share of big-budget studio pics. Sylvester Stallone worked for SAG scale in *Cop Land* (1997), just as Bruce Willis and John Travolta accepted a fraction of their usual salaries to appear in *Pulp Fiction*. TV actors (even those on the hottest sitcoms) often are eager to do a "little" film during their show's hiatus, in order to break out of a familiar role and to lay the groundwork for a leap to studio flicks. Other actors may not be offered substantial roles from the studios and would rather star in a small movie than play an insignificant role in a big one.

Furthermore, although an independent film may not have a lot of money to toss around, the pay is not necessarily woeful. On an indie with a budget of $1 million, a name actor could take home $100,000; not bad for five weeks of work. Even if the actor is performing for scale (as is commonly the case), the low-budget minimum is $1,620 per week plus ten percent (the ten percent goes to his agent). That's enough to pay most bills. Additionally, name actors usually receive a share in any eventual profits.

What matters most in attracting a respected actor is the script. If you can hook name talent with a great script, they may *have* to do it. This was the case with Harvey Keitel after reading *Reservoir Dogs:*

he read it, loved it and helped bring in more money and quality actors (for his efforts, he took a co-producer credit). It doesn't hurt to get your script to some "name" actors. If one of them commits your low-budget film suddenly won't be so low-budget anymore. Believe it: If Tom Cruise or Sandra Bullock commits, financing will materialize, your budget will grow and your once-little indie will be projected onto lots of screens.

However, getting a script to a celebrity is easier said than done. They often have a battalion of aides to protect them from such occurrences. Try to utilize any connections you may have however remote. If you don't have an inside route, call the celebrity's agent or manager (call the Screen Actors Guild or consult *Film Actors Guide*, which is published annually). Exaggerate a little about your budget and experience, and volunteer to send a script. Realize: the bigger the star, the harder it usually is to reach him. On the other hand, indie-friendly actors can sometimes be approached at film festivals, conferences and various industry events. Be polite and always respect the actor's right to ignore you.

The major Hollywood agencies—International Creative Management (ICM), Creative Artists Agency (CAA), William Morris and company are **packagers**. If you can sell one of these agencies on your project, they will represent you and the script and attach one or more of their name acting clients to it. Packaging allows the agency to take ten percent of the fees for the above-the-line talent (including you) and an additional fee of approximately five percent of the film's budget, plus net profit points. If this happens, your film likely won't be in the low-budget category anymore, you'll get paid handsomely and distribution will be all but guaranteed. This is a long shot for an inexperienced filmmaker, but it all comes down to that most important component: the script. A great screenplay can open otherwise locked doors. Anyway, it never hurts to knock.

Up to this point, "recognizable names" has been defined as well-known, quality actors who are perfect for a role. In other words: a director's dream. Now, let's turn to the producer's reality. Acting ability aside, low-budget films often have one name performer appearing in a small role. This is because any familiar face—even a has-been or pseudo-celebrity—will increase the video value of your film. The distributor will plaster their face on box covers to pump up sales, especially in foreign territories.

Name actors can make you money in the long run, but they may cost you in the short term. The reason some celebrities appear so briefly in low-budget projects is because they're getting a lot of money for very little work. For example, a celebrity may do a "walk-on" (one day of acting) in your little thriller, showing up as the ultimate transvestite killer, but for that one day this person may get fifty grand. The stiff fee will be set by the star's agent and will not be negotiable. Still, having said that, some has-beens are undoubtedly twiddling their thumbs and would love to do a movie for a reasonable paycheck.

As the director/producer, you must decide if you want a fading celebrity in your dream project. Can you afford to put up the extra money now to see it (hopefully) returned with interest later? The answer is probably "yes," if having that actor means significant financing. If it means only an eventual video sale, the question is more complex. Will the actor's inflated salary disrupt your cast and crew? Will his presence throw your story out of kilter or cheapen your film? William "The Refrigerator" Perry might be a tad distracting in an Elizabethan drama.

Paying for a pseudo-celebrity is a judgment call. In straight-to-video exploitation pictures, a name or two (regardless of ability) is almost a necessity. In a quirky little Sundance hopeful, consider it, but don't let it divert you from making the highest quality film possible.

SAG

In the past, the Screen Actors Guild (SAG), which represents most American film and TV actors of note, has had a rocky relationship with independent filmmakers. However, with the rising visibility and prestige of indies during recent years, SAG has loosened up and has made it less painful for low-budget productions to hire guild actors.

SAG imposes its **Basic Agreement** on films with budgets of more than $2 million. This sets a minimum pay requirement of $1,876 per five-day week ($540 per single day) for all actors in a film, plus pension and health contributions, plus a variety of rules and regulations. There is also a **Low-Budget Agreement** for movies budgeted between $500,000 and $2 million. The minimum salary is $1,620 per five-day week ($466 per day), plus pension and health contributions, rules and regulations. As you can see, this doesn't save you much. Thankfully, as of late 1996, SAG has created a **Modified Low-Budget Agreement** for films budgeted at less than $500,000. This cuts the rate down to a more manageable $864 per five-day week ($248 per day), plus pension and health and rules and regulations. The best part of these Agreements is that they include a theatrical buy out, meaning you have the right to screen your completed film for profit on North American screens. Residuals only have to be paid when the film goes to foreign markets, video and television.

But wait a minute. If you're a micro-budget filmmaker, even the Modified Low-Budget Agreement can seem pretty steep. What if you have a production budget of $40,000 and you need seven actors for three weeks of shooting? Let's do the math:

7 x 3 x $864 = $18,144.

The bottom line is still daunting.

SAG now has created a new and improved **Limited Exhibition Agreement**, which can be used by all films (it used to be limited to shorts) with budgets less than $200,000. It requires that you pay actors a minimum of $75 per day if they work three or more consecutive days ($100 per day for less than three consecutive days), plus overtime. You then have the right to screen your film at festivals and for distributors. According to this contract, if (and only if) you obtain commercial distribution, you (or, more likely, your distributor) then will be required to pay regular guild low-budget minimums to all actors.

The Modified Low-Budget Agreement and Limited Exhibition Agreement are positives for low-budget filmmakers. On the downside, SAG still has its rules. And, the worst of these—from an indie producer's point of view—is **overtime**. This clicks in when an actor is on the job for more than eight hours in a day or more than six days in a week (both common occurrences). Only a few hours of overtime can mean having to pay *triple* an actor's hourly wage! Similarly, penalties are assessed if an actor has less than twelve-hours of turnaround time between wrapping one day and his call time the next day. As your crew members may be working on a ten-hour turnaround (see: "CREW"), this can cause scheduling problems.

Studio productions often budget for overtime and turnaround penalties, but you may not be able to afford this luxury. To avoid excess costs, your assistant director should be an expert at juggling call times and wrap times (staggering them so that, for example, the first actor called is the first actor to wrap for the day). **Exhibit G's** are the SAG forms which (at least supposedly) keep close track of an actor's job time.

To become a SAG film, the production must first become a guild **signatory**. Begin this process as soon as possible because the steps sometimes take weeks to complete. You need to submit a budget to your SAG representative; in return, you will receive a stack of paperwork to fill out and sign. (One of the trickier matters is the **UCC form**, which allows the guild to take a financial interest in your screenplay if you cannot pay your actors. To execute the UCC, you'll need properly signed agreements with your writer and a script copyright from the Library of Congress. This takes a while.)

In addition, you'll be required to post a **SAG bond**. The cost of this approaches the total sum of all your actors' salaries. And it won't be returned until well into post-production (SAG will let it sit comfortably in an interest-bearing account). Therefore, you must plan for this (often huge) outlay in your cash flow.

When utilizing SAG actors, everyone with a speaking line must be in good standing with the guild. To employ a non-guild performer, you will have to **Taft-Hartley** him by filling out documentation that allows him to be employed for thirty days at guild rates without joining the guild. However, if someone has already been Taft-Hartleyed once (more than thirty days prior to the last day they're scheduled to appear in your film), SAG will now demand that they join the guild (and pay the guild's large initial fee) or not work for you. Once straightened out, everyone who speaks on-camera, SAG or not, must receive at least SAG minimum pay and be eligible for overtime and other panalties.

NON-SAG

SAG actors are now accessible to most independent filmmakers. But hold on. Remember the scary math—the seven actors working for three six-day weeks (ignore overtime) on your budget of $40,000. Even with a Limited Exhibition Agreement, at $75 per day, salaries will set you back $9,450—nearly one-quarter of your budget. What if you can't pay $75 per day per actor? What if you can't tiptoe around the various work requirements? What if you plan to cast only your family and friends or a few non-SAG stage actors? The truth is, although SAG has become more accessible in recent years, in some micro-budget situations, it still may be untenable. Don't fear. Many performers, including many members of SAG, will be knocking on your non-SAG door.

If you find yourself casting SAG actors, let them worry about their guild's regulations. Some may want to alter their names; if they get caught, they may be fined or excised from the guild. If you are a SAG member and you get nabbed, you will probably be fined. Robert Townsend, who was in SAG when *Hollywood Shuffle* was released, was called before a SAG review board and made to retroactively pay his actors guild minimums. If you're not in SAG, all they can do is bruise your reputation. The important thing is to not openly court guild actors for a non-guild production. Always specify non-SAG and don't ask too many questions about who may or may not be paying dues.

So, if you choose to not deal with SAG contracts and salary requirements, then why pay actors anything? It is true that there will be no shortage of performers willing to appear in your flick for free. No doubt, some of the more desperate, driven, and deranged would even pay you for a break (and some low-budget filmmakers have actually charged actors to be in their movies). If you just don't have the funds, make salaries deferred or, better yet, offer the old standby: "credit, meals and copy" and gas money.

On the other hand, if you can find a thousand dollars or so, it's best to pay your cast members something—even if it's just $20 to $40 per day. Also, add a few extra bucks for rehearsals (to cover transportation expenses). No people are more important to the success of your motion picture than the actors. Treat them well. Besides, a little cash will attract a more talented pool of recruits. Many SAG performers who won't consider deferred salaries will take any job "with pay"—even extremely low pay. Salaries separate you from student films and charities. They make your production professional, and professional actors will want to work for you.

To protect your budget, pay by the day, not the hour. Your days may be much longer than eight hours. Overtime will not be an option.

After being hired, all actors should sign a contract specifying their pay and duties; they should also sign a release form allowing you to utilize their likeness in various ways (see "PAPERWORK: Releases").

MINORS

If possible, avoid casting anyone below the age of eighteen, whether you're dealing with SAG or non-SAG actors. If you need to cast for a teenager, try to hire a legal adult who can play a younger character. If you must cast a child in your film, you will have to deal with an abundance of child labor laws. These vary from state to state, but they'll all limit (often severely) the amount of time a child can work on your film. Labor agencies also mandate various educational requirements and demand that a parent or guardian and a representative from the Labor or Education Department be nearby at all times. School tutoring rules are sometimes in effect even when school is out for the summer.

Of course, some stories need child actors. *Kids* and *Welcome to the Dollhouse* both employed minors in principal roles. In fact, *Welcome to the Dollhouse* utilized more than 500 underage extras and was made for $700,000. So, it can be done. (*Welcome to the Dollhouse* was limited to five-day weeks by child labor laws, but the production avoided New Jersey tutoring requirements by filming in the summer.)

If you must cast a child as a principal player, contact your local or state Department of Labor. Also, make sure the child's parents approve everything in your script. You don't want the mom and dad suddenly pulling their child in the middle of your production because they disapprove of the theme or plot.

EXTRAS

You may be able to get your friends and family—as well as production assistants or anyone interested in a first credit—to appear as extras in a scene for nothing but meals, credit and gas money. But beware: free workers can flake out. Treat them with respect and make them feel comfortable. If your background talent must be on-call for more than one day, make sure they're reliable. Relatives, good friends and those already involved with the production are best. If you're using outside volunteers, have other options lined up in case they decide not to show up.

Larger independent productions hire professional extras and pay appropriate salaries (around $75 per day).

REHEARSALS

As was mentioned earlier, one of the advantages of working with non-stars is that you can schedule full rehearsals for little or no pay. Inexperienced actors will need all the practice they can get. Also, if you're an inexperienced filmmaker, these sessions will help you sharpen your directing skills.

Actors react to rehearsals differently: some like them, some don't, some go all out, some hold back for the shoot. And, practice doesn't always make perfect. As the director, a key facet of your job is to discern each performer's optimum working methodology and to guide him accordingly.

The danger with scheduling too many rehearsals is that moments meant to be spontaneous can sometimes become routine. Be aware of this possibility. If your actors appear listless, stop rehearsing, lighten the schedule or shake things up (costumes, new location, outside observers . . .) to keep the vitality.

The first rehearsal should be a full-cast **read-through** of the script so that each actor can get a feel for his role in relation to his fellow performers. Even big-budget studio films do this (although it is sometimes all they do). As the name suggests, a read-through is "on-book" (un-memorized). This is the time, before the lines are memorized, for you and your cast to make sure you're in agreement on the content and delivery of all dialogue.

As the rehearsal schedule progresses and you move closer to production, the actors should be able to go more and more "off-book" (memorized). This will be of greater importance to your indie film than to a studio picture because of the limited number of takes you'll be shooting. Repeatedly muffed lines or bad readings are costly when the camera is rolling. Be especially aware of any stretches of dialogue that you plan to cover in extended shots. As a general rule, the sooner actors learn their lines, the more they can concentrate on their delivery. Memorization breeds confidence and confidence is a paramount quality in acting.

Because movies are usually shot out of sequence, it's generally helpful for you and the actors to do some in-sequence rehearsing, like a stage play. Rehearsals can be anywhere, even in your home, but it's ideal if they can be staged at the actual location or in a similar environment. In addition to giving the actors a sense of their surroundings, it allows you to **block** (plan the spacing of) all movements.

Acting is a process in constant flux. Try to let your performers discover their characters on their own. Give them confidence; allow them to grow. They may come up with things that surprise you. Go with what works best—it's usually that which seems most "natural" (i.e., doesn't feel like acting). Have an open mind and be willing to adopt new interpretations. But don't let an impressive line reading, action or emotion distract you from your overall vision. It's your job to focus everyone toward the greater good of the film.

As always, remain in control at rehearsals. Try to encourage a sense of family and teamwork. The relationships built now between the director and the actors and the actors with each other will carry over when the camera starts rolling.

One of the final preproduction sessions should be a **dress rehearsal** in full wardrobe and on an actual set. This gives everyone a feel for costumes, props and surroundings. It will also allow you to do more precise blocking, to determine where performers should be in relation to each other and the camera.

Rehearsals don't end when the camera starts rolling. Production rehearsals will be discussed in "MAKING A MOVIE: Speed."

8/CREW

Where do you find talented crew people willing to work for what you're able to pay? Believe it or not, they're out there and there's no shortage of them. In fact, they're probably slaving away—or clamoring to slave away—on an indie production right now. There are several ways to bring these people to your attention.

You can post **crew notices** for free in casting papers like *Drama-Logue* or *BackStage* or for a fee in other publications. You might try the Internet; depending on the site, you may be able to post jobs there for free. Similar to placing an ad for actors, specify the dates of the shoot and if there is pay. As with casting, **word of mouth** will travel through the production community, especially when you have a listing in the trade papers (see "PUBLICITY, PART 1: Spreading the Word, Part 1").

At this point, you should be aware of the many fine **organizations** that support independent filmmakers, including:

- Independent Feature Project (IFP), with regional branches in New York, Los Angeles, Chicago, Minneapolis, and Florida;

- Association of Independent Video and Filmmakers (AIVF) in N.Y.C.;

- Film Arts Foundation in San Francisco;

- Black Filmmakers Foundation in L.A. and N.Y.C.;

- Filmmakers Foundation in L.A.;

- International Documentary Association (IDA) in L.A.

Among the varied services these groups offer their members (including discounts on items like insurance) are job banks or bulletin boards filled with resumés of experienced crew members willing to work hard for indie wages (i.e. pitiful pay).

Any **college** with film or video production classes will have potential grips, electricians, assistant directors, boom operators and p.a.'s—all of whom usually are willing to work on the cheap. Any school with an art department should have students who can provide production design services. Similarly, a cosmetology school is where you might find low-cost (or even free) make-up and hair specialists; a fashion institute may provide your wardrobe crew.

Most importantly, the independent film scene thrives on **recommendations**. Somebody always knows somebody else who will work hard for $60 per fourteen-hour day. These aren't masochists; they're people who realize that, in the entertainment world, recommendations are rungs on the career ladder. They'll work hard now, going from low-paying gig to low-paying gig, in order to step up the ladder to higher-paying jobs tomorrow. A good production manager has a Rolodex full of competent low-salary crew people. Also, once you hire one experienced person, he often will be able to recommend people for other positions. In this way, hard-working crews sometimes move nearly intact from one film to another.

Check resumés and references. While interviewing is primarily the job of the u.p.m. and/or producer, on small films, the director usually has final say, and the cinematographer may hire the people who will work directly under him (camera assistants, gaffer and key grip). The only people you can perhaps hire without a formal interview are production assistants (on low-budget films, they usually work for free).

When interviewing, check for attitude problems. Make sure everyone is committed to making the motion picture the way YOU want it made. And be certain they're willing to work for long hours under your probable working conditions. Be honest. You don't want people quitting while you're in the middle of directing your eighteenth straight hour in triple-digit heat.

Spell out salaries and duties in contracts which refer to each crew person as an "independent contractor." As with non-SAG actors, the pay for crew members should be computed by the day (not the hour), even if you originally negotiate a total sum for the entire shoot. Avoid the word "overtime." Salaries are generally paid at the end of each week.

As stated earlier, don't defer salaries unless it's absolutely necessary. Most *experienced* crew people will balk at deferred pay and an *experienced* crew is what you'll need for a fast, efficient production.

Treat your crew well. Morale problems can be created by difficult working conditions, or by something as simple as a bad meal or an understocked craft service table (see: "FOOD"). Remember: free meals are part of everyone's salary.

Another important factor for maintaining crew morale is to keep at least a **ten-hour turnaround** between one day's wrap and the next day's call. For example, if you wrap at 11:00 p.m. on Monday, the first call on Tuesday should be no earlier than 9:00 a.m. The turnaround time should be longer if there's a lengthy commute. If you work more than fourteen hours in a day (which is not uncommon) and you adhere to the ten-hour turnaround time, you'll be pushing call times back as the week goes on. However, your off-days (usually Sundays) will serve as a natural stop to this procedure. (A ten-hour turnaround might force you to have a 1:00 p.m. call on a Saturday, but, with Sunday off, you can start again with a 7:00 a.m. Monday call.) As the director working on adrenaline, you might be able to go three weeks straight on three hours of sleep per night, but your crew will not. And they shouldn't have to.

Similar to SAG, which protects the actors, crew unions serve a useful function in protecting workers' rights, but, like SAG, they can add heavily to your budget. Even bigger films, such as the $7 million *Pulp Fiction*, were made without union crews. If you employ one member of the International Alliance of Theatrical Stage Employees (IATSE), which may include your favorite cinematographer or production designer, everyone else you hire is supposed to be in a union; this means stiff salaries and strict work requirements for all.

One of the worst aspects of utilizing union crews is the compartmentalizing of jobs. For instance, a camera assistant cannot move a light; a sound technician can't pull a camera cable. On a big studio film, this procedure ensures that the right person is performing the correct job. But with a low-budget film utilizing a small crew, this can be restrictive. Independent film shoots should promote a family atmosphere in which everyone can and will help everyone else. Try to avoid working with the unions.

WRITER, DIRECTOR, & PRODUCER

The duties of the writer, director and producer are defined throughout this book. If you perform one or more of these roles and you're lucky enough to get substantial outside financing, pencil in an adequate (but not outrageous) salary for yourself; two to four percent of the overall budget is fair. On the other hand, if you're financing the film yourself, perhaps with the help of family and friends, or if you have only meager outside financing, brace yourself. Not only will you NOT make money up-front; not only will you NOT give yourself a salary; not only will you NOT see a cent during the many months of writing, planning, shooting, editing and selling, but you're probably going to spend every penny (or almost every penny) you have. You may go into debt.

So, what's in it for you? Where's you slice of the money pie? You, the creator, the leader, the person who's been dreaming about this for years, putting everything you have into it, working the hardest and longest? Your pay comes in two ways.

First, you share in any profits if—*and this is a big "if"*—there are any profits. If you're the person putting up the cash yourself, you will receive most, if not all, of the producer's return. If outside investors are helping you, they'll take their slice, but you'll still get a chunk. If you're a writer, director or producer and you're working entirely with someone else's funds but you can't wrangle yourself a salary, then you should get **net profit points** (three to ten points is typical, depending on your role). One net profit point equals one percent of any profits. Potentially, points can pay off like a Vegas jackpot, but most times you won't even get a coin back.

The second (and more important) way you get paid is in your future earnings, via the screen credit you receive and the promise of a brighter tomorrow. Looking at the big picture, writing, directing or producing a feature film is a tremendous credit on your resumé. And, even if your project does not turn a profit, if it is noticed by just one person who matters, it could launch your career towards potentially huge paydays.

One more thing. You become a member of the Writers Guild of America (WGA) by selling your script for at least the guild minimum to a WGA member company. You join the Directors Guild of America (DGA) by directing a guild-registered production (as well as through a long process of assistant directing and production managing). There is essentially no producer's guild.

MORE PRODUCERS

Occasionally, a respected filmmaker with a lot of clout, like Spike Lee or Martin Scorsese, will attach his name to an independent film and shepherd it through to distribution. In a case like this, they will probably take the title of **Executive Producer**. Likewise, if a distributor gets involved early, the executives there may slap their names onto the above-the-line credits. If either of these things happen, great, your biggest problems—money and distribution—are probably solved. However, for the most part, executive producer credits on independent features go to heavy investors (those who contribute more than twenty-five percent of the budget) and/or to the people who bring in the heavy investors. For this work, they'll receive an executive producer credit and a big slice of any profits (see "MONEY: Investors"). Try to minimize or contractually eliminate the creative control of such people.

The **Associate Producer** credit, for your purposes, is usually reserved for hard-working folks (production manager, writer, etc.) who make contributions above and beyond their routine duties. **Line Producer** is an inflated way of saying Unit Production Manager. These job titles are set apart because, as opposed to the u.p.m. or assistant director, they usually will appear in the film's front credits and may also show up in print advertising, posters, press releases and on video boxes.

Treat credits like currency: spend them wisely. Use "inflated" credits in a limited fashion in lieu of up-front salaries and often in conjunction with deferred pay or profit points. Don't just hand out titles to friends: the more producer credits there are, the less value they have. So, reserve them for those who truly earn them. Some u.p.m.'s working for free will deserve a full producer credit; some quality casting directors, writers, production designers, etc., will toil away for little or nothing if given an associate producer credit.

UNIT PRODUCTION MANAGER & ASSISTANT DIRECTOR

As was mentioned previously, on nonstudio productions, **unit production manager** (u.p.m.) and line producer are essentially the same. The difference is that a line producer credit is more prestigious. Whatever the title, before a shoot, the u.p.m. will be busy. In addition to budgeting and scheduling the production, he is responsible (in conjunction with the producers) for securing the crew, making all purchases and rentals, and handling such items as permits, releases, insurance and contracts. During production, the u.p.m. will pay the bills, secure equipment and stock and take care of any necessary paperwork. On larger movies, at least one **production coordinator** will assist the u.p.m. On low-budget shoots, the u.p.m.'s duties sometimes are absorbed by the producer.

When the budget is slim, the unit production manager and the assistant director are sometimes one and the same. The u.p.m./a.d. will work on budgeting, crewing, paperwork, etc., during preproduction and then serve as assistant director during production; at this time, the producer will assume the u.p.m.'s role.

The **1st assistant director** (1st a.d.) comes on-board during preproduction to assist the director in organizing the shooting schedule. During production, the 1st a.d. is responsible for running the set efficiently, keeping the shoot on-schedule, juggling call times and wrap times and generally making sure everyone performs his job. The a.d. also handles production paperwork. (For example, if you're "going SAG," the a.d. will be charged with filling out the Exhibit G forms and keeping track of SAG's regulations.) Find an assistant director with significant experience, who is likable but firm. Your a.d. will need to have the respect of the crew for your shoot to run smoothly.

Second and **2nd 2nd assistant directors** will assist the 1st a.d. and the u.p.m. (or producer) with production paperwork, legwork and phone work. A 2nd a.d. usually is responsible for the call sheets, union forms and other off-set matters, thus leaving the 1st a.d. to run the set. On micro-budget films, 2nd assistant directors will probably be production assistants willing to work for free as long as their job title has the word "director" in it. (See also "MAKING A MOVIE: Assistant Directing.")

CINEMATOGRAPHER & ASSISTANTS

The **cinematographer** (also known as the director of photography or d.p.) is one of the most critical positions you will fill. He is usually the best paid of your below-the-line crew—and for good reason. The d.p. is responsible, in conjunction with the director, for the movie's visual look.

Do not settle for a beginner. Cinematography is an art and a skill mastered through experience. Hire someone with proven abilities who has shot a film under circumstances and budgetary constraints similar to your production.

Carefully view the reels of prospective cinematographers. If necessary, watch their work without sound. You may also want to slow down or pause certain sections to study the contents of the frame. Beware of flashy, quick-cut action backed up by thumping music: you may be responding to the MTV glitz, editing and tunes—not the cinematography. Instead, look for proper framing, lighting, focus and camera movement. Pay special attention to how close-ups are rendered.

A variety of credits is a plus, but make sure the prospective cinematographers have worked previously in your film format. When calling references, inquire as to how easily the cinematographer got along with others and how fast he was able to execute setups with a small crew. Most importantly, after he has had an opportunity to read your script, make sure the two of you are on the same page—that you share the same goals for the film's look and that you have a good and easy rapport.

The earlier the cinematographer can begin work, the better. During preproduction, he can help scout locations, assemble the crew and prepare the shooting strategy.

On a low-budget feature, the d.p. will often operate the camera. On a higher-budget film, this duty will be assumed by the **camera operator** or the **first assistant camera** person (1st a.c.). Whether or not he is behind the camera, the 1st a.c. also will be responsible for changing lenses and filters, setting the focus and keeping the lenses and gates clean. (Regularly checking to make sure the camera gate is clean is especially important with 16mm or Super 16mm film formats because the subsequent blow-up can make a stray eyelash look like an anaconda.)

The **second assistant camera** person (2nd a.c.) will load and unload film, complete camera department paperwork and (probably) slate each take (done with an electronically timed clapboard). On smaller productions, the grip might slate; larger shoots often have a **loader** handling the film stock. Loading film into magazines is a major duty (manipulated within a lightproof, zippered bag), especially when shooting with short ends (short, cheaper rolls).

The cinematographer usually hires the camera assistants; often he works with the same people regularly. No matter who hires for these positions, it's best to get energetic people who have significant experience in your film format; inexperienced camera assistants can cost you significant chunks of time or, even worse, exposed film.

EDITOR

There will be much more about picture editing later (in the appropriately titled "PICTURE EDITING" section), but your **editor** should be hired during preproduction so that he can begin assembling footage while you are in production. Even very low-budget films should find an experienced editor who has previously cut at least one full-length feature. Watch the reels of prospective editors, but understand that even a bad editor is usually competent at stringing together scenes or sequences. Of more importance is this person's ability to tell a full-length story in a compelling manner. For this reason, try to watch one or two of his films in their entirety.

More than anyone else, the editor is a person you should be comfortable with: the two of you will be spending a lot of time together in (typically) close quarters. A potential editor should not show any ego or attitude because ultimately he needs to be acquiescent to your whims.

Typically, most films today are edited in a non-linear fashion, therefore, an **assistant editor** will not be mandatory. If you can afford the luxury of hiring an assistant editor, this person will perform such mundane tasks as digitizing video footage, inserting titles, keeping records and running assorted errands.

On the other hand, if you choose to edit your film in the "old-school" fashion—on a flatbed—one or two full-time assistants will be required to synch sound with picture and organize the many sections of developed film.

Your editor should be skilled at handling whatever computer editing system you've selected, i.e., *AVID, Lightworks, D-Vision,* etc. This means editing without assistance, without hesitation and without frequent technical support calls. Time, money and data can be lost if the editor must relearn or refresh his memory of key strokes, storage procedures, etc.

It is a tremendous advantage if your editor has connections to great equipment. Editors with allies can sometimes procure under-used editing systems for little or no money, especially during the wee hours of the morning. Without this connection, renting a system will be a major expense.

By the way, if those of you on a micro-budget opt for linear editing (see "PICTURE EDITING: Linear"), you probably won't need to hire an editor or assistant; nor will you need to rent any equipment. Sound great? It's cheap, but it's neither easy nor fast.

PRODUCTION DESIGN

A variety of roles fall under this category. The **production designer** (p.d.) works with the director to conceive, plan and supervise the look of the scenery, sets and props. The **art director** executes the design, answering to the p.d. The **set decorator** dresses the set. The **property master** (props) inventories and maintains all props and set dressings.

Major productions will fill all of the above design positions and several more (i.e., crew for set construction, a researcher, a graphic artist, etc.). On the other hand, on low-budget films, one or two people may be doing all these jobs—and then some. On micro-budget films that are shot entirely on location, you may not have any official design people: all such duties may be absorbed by the director, producer(s) and production assistants.

The best production designer is one who shares your visual ideas and who knows how to execute them at minimal cost. Your production designer should have decorating skills, a thorough understanding of cinematic framing and the ability to find bargains. Those with low-budget experience often have connections to art supply houses, thrift stores, etc., that can save you significant money (sometimes more than their salary).

Your shoot will probably need at least one individual to assist the production designer in dressing sets and handling props. It may also be this person's responsibility to take snapshots for set and props continuity. (An "art director" credit can serve as valuable currency here.)

SOUND

Low-budget movies are notorious for their poor sound quality. Don't contribute to the noise pollution! Get clear, correctly recorded audio during production or end up paying during post-production, struggling in vain to clean up sound mistakes.

The **sound mixer** is responsible for all production sound. This person mixes the volume levels for the microphones and tries to capture theater-quality audio. The mixer will usually have his own equipment and therefore he'll get paid twice: once for working and once for renting his equipment to the production. This is fair because he has a legitimate investment in his gear. However, when negotiating his pay, lump the salary and rental fees together, making them sound as big as they are; for the opposite reason, he will prefer negotiating these items separately.

In an ideal world, the mixer will bring in an experienced **boom operator**. But low-budget filmmaking is not an ideal world. If you don't have the money, you may have to consider using a p.a. or film student for this job. But, be forewarned: Rookie boom operators make mistakes. You will probably end up seeing a boom microphone in the frame or hear a voice fade in and out. You and your d.p. should watch the frameline and the mixer should keep an eye on channel levels. Consider allowing your d.p. or sound mixer to say, "Cut!" if faulty mic work is ruining a shot. (See "MAKING A MOVIE: Sound.")

SCRIPT SUPERVISOR

The **script supervisor** takes the production notes, which include writing down the take numbers, camera positions, dialogue changes, running time and various other aspects of **continuity** (which are the details necessary for matching shots; see "MAKING A MOVIE: Continuity"). The supervisor's **script notes** will aid the director during production (was that apple on the desk in the last shot?) and the editor during post-production (was there another medium shot of that line?).

A good script supervisor is tireless and unfailingly observant. Hire the best person possible, but at the micro-budget level you may have to utilize a relatively inexperienced person looking to acquire credits. Still, make sure at least one previous director recommends this person.

Get a screenplay and shooting script to your script supervisor as soon as he is hired in order for him to become familiar with the dialogue and details of your story.

GAFFER & ELECTRICIANS

The **gaffer** works for the director of photography to execute the lighting. The d.p. often hires the gaffer and utilizes the same person on project after project. Make sure any prospective gaffer can fulfill your lighting vision (especially when working in black and white) and that he is fully prepared to toil within your budget and schedule and with your available equipment and crew.

Electricians (or electrics), including the **best boy** (chief electrician), work for the gaffer and cinematographer to adjust lights and move electrical equipment. Try to get experienced electricians, even if you have to pay a little more. A practiced, efficient crew will save you money in the long run by working faster with less problems. Also, paying the lighting crew a little bit more helps prevent desertions if a bigger film should come along.

GRIPS

The **key grip** works for the director of photography and supervises the grip crew. The **dolly grip** (on independent shoots, the key and dolly grips are often the same) moves the camera dolly. Get an experienced key/dolly grip who, like the gaffer, is fully prepared to work within your budget and schedule, with a possibly meager crew and with possibly less-than-ideal equipment.

In addition to a key/dolly grip, you'll need at least one additional grip. Grips are movers, so the more grips you have, the faster things go. Grips set up dolly tracks, lay down marks and they move almost everything: equipment, flats, cables, food tables . . . anything! They may also assist the electrical, art and camera departments (at least when working non-union). Good grips are tireless. Treat them well and they'll keep working hard.

When it comes to grips and electricians, make sure you have several potential alternates on your contact sheet. A film can screech to an abrupt halt if half of your grip crew (which may mean only one person!) calls in sick.

MAKE-UP & HAIR

Better-financed indies hire a **make-up artist** and a **make-up assistant**. Some micro-budget movies manage without either. If you absolutely do not have the funds and you have a small cast and you're shooting in black and white, you can get by with actors applying their own cosmetics. However, for most color productions it's best to find someone (perhaps someone just starting out and willing to work for food and credit) to make up your performers. Whatever your situation, allow for an appropriate amount of supplies in your budget.

Special make-up effects don't always require special skills. Stage blood and fake skin putty are available at most costume stores. And, if the screen time is limited, fake cuts, bullet holes, bloody noses, etc., aren't hard to pull off. After all, since the bargain basement blood-by-the-bucket days of Hershell Gordon Lewis (*2000 Maniacs* [1964]), thousands of low-budget movies have been splattered with fake blood. More advanced effects may require specialized technicians. (See "MAKING A MOVIE: Special Effects & Stunts.")

Not every movie can afford a **hair stylist**. On movies with a small cast and budget, the make-up artist or the actors themselves may need to style hair. If you have scenes featuring a large cast and/or unique hair, pay an outside stylist to work only on those particular "bad hair days." (By the way, actors with very short hair or shaved heads will need to maintain their cuts closely over a multiple-week shoot, lest they cause continuity problems. Budget for haircuts.)

WARDROBE

Some indie films (especially those set in any time but the present) need a full-time **costume designer** or **wardrobe master** and assistants. For those of you on low budgets, try to find someone (perhaps for screen credit only) who will show up late in the rehearsal stage to advise you of appropriate fashions. If you do not have the funds and you cannot find anyone to work for little or no money and if your cast members are wearing their own threads, you can manage without a wardrobe department.

An experienced low-budget wardrober should be able to save you money by finding cheap clothes and/or highlighting appropriate items in your actors' closets. Set aside some cash for purchases.

The production will probably need to launder clothing. Budget for **professional cleaning** and assign the delivery and pickup to someone (wardrobe assistant, p.a.). If you leave it to actors to wash what they wear—considering the lack of time they'll have during a typically hectic low-budget shooting schedule—you'll wind up with performers not looking (or smelling) their best.

PRODUCTION ASSISTANTS

With a job only slightly more prestigious than rowing on a galley ship, a **production assistant** (p.a.) on an independent film (whether the budget is $20,000 or $2,000,000) is most likely an intern and will not collect a salary. Instead, he works for food, a screen credit, probably a gas allowance and, most importantly, the exalting thrill of being employed in the "glamorous world" of motion picture production.

The p.a. job is a learning experience (he'll learn he doesn't want to be a p.a. anymore!) and he will do any job that needs to be done. You should have several on your shoot: they don't need to work full-time and can rotate days.

Production assistants can be found among your family and friends (let's hope they're still your friends after you've asked them to do a few hundred menial chores), through crew listings or at film schools. They may be people striving to be grips or designers or directors or actors. They can be anyone, anywhere. Treat them with respect at all times and show your appreciation. Devoid of money, the glamour fades fast.

9/FOOD

Food will be one of the most important (and expensive) line items of your production budget. Always provide delicious, hot meals. There also should be adequate snacks and beverages available throughout the day (the job of **Craft Services**). Ideally, food should be dished out in a comfortable eating area, complete with tables and chairs. Meals should be served at least every six hours; meal breaks should last at least one-half hour. Experienced employees in the entertainment industry (union or nonunion) expect these rules to be strictly adhered to.

In the morning, cereals and light pastries—with plenty of hot coffee—should be laid out on the craft-service table. An adequate supply of fruit and an assortment of vitamins (especially vitamin C) are smart moves in order to maintain your crew's health; illness costs time and money.

Six hours after the first call, you should serve a catered meal. Shop for the right food service. Almost any **caterer** (not necessarily one who works exclusively in the entertainment industry) will be happy to serve your production if the price is right. To save money, you may find a caterer just starting out who is hungry for business. But be prudent. Look at sample menus that cover the entire shooting schedule; prospective caterers should be able to tell you in advance exactly what they'll be serving for each of your production days. Ask to sample some of their cooking. Check references for unanimous praise.

Before the first day of production, find out if any crew members have special dietary needs (i.e., allergies to specific foods, vegetarian requests, etc.). Ensure that appropriate food is prepared for them and that there is sufficient variety from meal to meal.

Micro-budget shoots sometimes cook their own meals. Director Ed Burns's mom "catered" *The Brothers McMullen* from her own kitchen (much of the film was shot in the family house). While home-style cooking is often the best, go this route only if your (tiny) crew is made up of your family and friends and if you have the facilities and chef(s) to serve everyone hot, quality meals in a timely fashion. Otherwise, if things fail to go according to menu, you'll be faced with grumbling stomachs and grouchy employees.

Assuming your cast and crew is small, you can buy each day's meals from local restaurants. This is not always cheaper, and it can be a logistical nightmare. Nevertheless, it is an option you may want to explore. If you go this route, make sure there's a different type of food everyday and that there is more than one choice of entree for each meal. By promising to thank the restaurants in your screen credits, you may be able to wrangle discounts or even—outside of L.A. and New York—free cuisine.

If you're still working six hours after the first catered meal, it will be time for a second spread. On nonstudio flicks, the second meal usually is not fully catered; it either is bought from a local restaurant or cooked in-house.

If you're working six hours after the second catered meal (more than nineteen hours after the first call), wow . . . well, it does happen. It'll probably be time for breakfast again. Lots of coffee!

Throughout the day, cold and hot drinks and plenty of snacks should be available on the craft service table. You'll need ice, a small refrigerator or ice chests and a heavy-duty coffeemaker. A prudent shopper (if not an official **craft services person,** then perhaps the u.p.m. or one of the p.a.'s) should be in charge of buying for and stocking the craft service table. Probably, this person also will be responsible for picking up and laying out any meals not prepared by a caterer.

Feed your people well. Food is fuel.

10/STOCK

On big productions, the cost of film stock is a mere blip in the budget. In all likelihood, major studio flicks could expose film nonstop throughout production and the cost still wouldn't be as high as the salary of the second lead. But, in the world of scrounging and scraping, stock will be one of the largest components of your slim budget. Luckily, there are ways to save.

BLACK & WHITE, COLOR
The decision to shoot in either **black and white** (B&W) or **color** will not significantly affect stock prices, but black and white film is cheaper to process and to print. Additionally, it is generally quicker to light for B&W film (remember: time is money) and the final results often hide low-budget flaws in design and makeup better than color film. These features may allow you to get by with a smaller (cheaper) crew and a tighter (cheaper) schedule.

When it comes to shooting in B&W, keep in mind that although you can save cash up-front, you may lose it on the back end because movies in black and white have been deemed less commercially viable than films in color. This is especially true for video sales. Director Michael Corrente made his first film, *Federal Hill* (1994), an $80,000 indie, in B&W but it was later shamelessly *colorized* by Trimark, its distributor! The director and d.p. had to fight to have it released not in the pallid primary colors and sickly flesh tones of colorization but as it was originally conceived and shot. This defilement aside, the independent film scene is the one place where movies made in shades of gray, like *Stranger Than Paradise* (1984),

She's Gotta Have It (1986) and *Clerks* (1994), are almost always accepted as equals with their chromatic brothers.

Don't opt for black and white solely because of economics. After all, the no-budget indie *El Mariachi* (1993) was filmed in color while the big-budget studio film *Schindler's List* (1993) was not. The decision to shoot in B&W should be primarily an aesthetic one, dictated by your story. Some intimate or downbeat stories may feel gray and therefore translate well in B&W, but to capture life's rich pageantry, most movies should color.

Beware: If you opt for the less-traveled black and white path, make sure your cinematographer and gaffer have experience lighting it and that your lab is adept at processing it.

35MM, SUPER 16MM, 16MM, VIDEO

After you settle the color / no-color question, you still have decisions to make on the type of stock you'll shoot with. However, size format choices are primarily dictated by your budget.

The ideal stock is **35mm**. After all, discounting the occasional big-budget 70mm or Super 35mm print, every motion picture that is released theatrically is released in 35mm. But shooting in 35mm will be expensive.

- The film stock itself is expensive (four times as much per minute as 16mm).

- The camera package is expensive to rent (twice as much as 16mm).

- The lab costs are expensive (three times as much as 16mm).

If your total budget is more than $170,000, you can porobably squeeze 35mm prices into the stock, equipment and lab categories. If the figures won't fit without major sacrifices, or if your budget is less than $170,000, read on:

Most feature-length festival films budgeted at less than $170,000 opt to film in **Super 16mm.** Then, in post-production, they try to get extra funding to blow up the print to 35mm. Super 16 is virtually the same aspect ratio (relative dimensions) as 35mm; therefore, when optically doubled and transferred to 35mm, Super 16 resembles the full rectangle of a major motion picture (albeit a somewhat grainy one). This makes it more appealing to potential theatrical distributors than the squarer shape of a 16mm film.

The main drawback to Super 16 is that, outside of laboratories, projectors for this format are virtually nonexistent. Therefore, Super 16 films cannot be publicly screened (except on videotape) until they're blown up to 35mm. This costs an additional $40,000 or more. If you can't come up with the money, you've made a film that will never be properly seen.

By the way, some directors who could shoot in 35mm prefer to shoot in Super 16 and then blow up the print because the lighter, more mobile camera better suits their coverage. Mike Figgis opted to shoot *Leaving Las Vegas* (made in 1995 for $3.5 million) in Super 16; Spike Lee made the same decision for his $2 million film, *Get On The Bus*, 1996.

Regular 16mm is squarer than 35mm or Super 16 and blows up into the shape of a TV-like box. Its dimensions make the stock less appealing for theatrical distribution, but don't hurt its chances of being sold to TV or for video distribution. Regular 16 is only slightly cheaper to buy and process than Super 16. You may, however, be able to save money on the equipment, as 16mm cameras are quite common (some cinematographers even own their own).

Regular 16's biggest advantage over Super 16 is that, because projectors are common (even high schools and prisons have them), you can easily show your movie on a big screen at festivals or to distributors before getting any completion funds (which will allow you to blow up the print to 35mm). A significant number of micro-budget successes were shot on regular 16 before being blown up, including *Clerks*, *Slacker* and *The Brothers McMullen*. Most independent documentaries are in this format. Short films, which are rarely blown up, should almost always be shot in regular 16 in order to be easily screened.

Something else to consider is that 16mm cameras can have the top and bottom of the picture frame masked so that the developed image resembles the aspect ratio of 35mm. This allows you to shoot in 16mm and screen with 16mm projectors, but you will have a product that, when blown up, will look like a 35mm film. The disadvantage to this is that by reducing the already-small 16mm frame, you'll have to blow up the film even more to get it to 35mm, thus making the finished product appear more grainy (and maybe less appealing) to distributors.

Video (preferably Beta SP, although Hi-8 and even Super VHS have been used on micro-micro shoots) is often used when making a movie for less (sometimes much less) than $40,000. Typically, exploitation or action-oriented films are made in this format; they are then sold directly to (mostly foreign) video markets. In a twist on the blow-up blues, grain is often *added* to a film shot on video, to give it a more filmlike quality. Though not a good strategy for getting noticed at festivals or by film distributors, making any movie (even in video) will give you valuable experience and you can earn a small profit by making a straight-to-video action-fest. Most of the same rules that apply to budgeting, casting, crewing and shooting a $350,000 feature film apply to a $35,000 straight-to-video exploitation flick.

Also consider that a film shot in broadcast-quality video can be blown up to 35mm film and screened in theaters; this was the route taken by the highly praised 1994 documentary *Hoop Dreams*. Since that landmark film, more documentaries have gone this route, including 1996's *Paradise Lost*. In a twist on this method, *Breaking the Waves* (1996), the Danish Oscar-nominated feature, was shot in Super 35 by director Lars Von Trier, who then transferred it to video and then back to regular 35mm in order to wash out colors and texture and give the film a bleaker look.

In the future, more motion pictures likely will adopt pre-film formats, especially when we have the ability to record easily on digital stock. But, as of this writing, if you want to make a festival-friendly narrative feature, go with film.

COMPUTING
Basic movie math:

- Lesson #1: Ninety feet of 35mm film equals one minute; 8,100 feet equals a ninety-minute feature.

- Lesson #2: Thirty-six feet of 16mm or Super 16 film equals one minute; 3,240 feet equals a ninety-minute feature.

- Lesson #3: When comparing film costs, remember to budget in the lab processing fees and not just the negative film prices. All coverage being equal, there will be two times as much 35mm film to process as 16mm or Super 16mm film.

- Lesson #4: In all but the most special of circumstances, your shooting ratio should be at least 5:1—film stock to running time. That's not five takes for the actors. You'll burn up film for leaders, slates, etc., and things will go wrong technically. A shooting ratio of 5:1 suddenly will drop to 4:1 (if not 3:1) without you even noticing. Then you'll want to cover dialogue from more than one angle, from more than one distance, with more than one line reading. Someone will miss his mark or a line will be flubbed. And then the camera won't be in perfect focus or the dolly move will be less than smooth. And then a line will be flubbed again. A ratio of 10:1 is more realistic. The higher the shooting ratio, the better.

Extra film (which gives you extra takes) is the best reason for shooting in Super 16mm or regular 16mm. If your choice is between shooting 4:1 in 35mm on a fourteen-day schedule or 10:1 in Super 16mm on a twenty-two-day schedule, there's no choice: even with some blow-up graininess, you'll make a much better movie in Super 16mm—with dialogue covered from three different angles and three takes of each shot—than if you compromise your vision and limit your coverage options to get it in the can in a pristine 35mm print. This is the kind of choice you'll have to make with a budget between $100,000 and $300,000.

Swimming with Sharks (made for $250,000 in 1994) was shot in 35mm, supposedly at an amazingly low 3:1 ratio, on an eighteen-day schedule (and at basically two locations), but this is a rare exception to lesson #4. Besides, it might have been a better movie with more coverage, locations and shooting days, but we'll never know. Don't shoot in 35mm if it means severely restricting your coverage.

- Lesson #5: How much stock do you buy? Compute the estimated time of your film. This will be approximately the same as the total number of pages in your (non-shooting) script (one page generally equals one minute). For more accurate timing, watch the clock while you read the screenplay and act out movements. Your script supervisor should be expert at doing this. Multiply the running time by 90 (for 35mm stock) or by 36 (for 16mm or Super 16mm stock). Then multiply this amount by your projected shooting ratio. The total will be the amount of film stock you'll need to buy. A 100-minute movie shot in Super 16mm, at an 8:1 ratio, will be computed as such:

100 x 36 x 8 = 28,800

This production will need 28,800 feet of negative stock.

SHOPPING FOR FILM STOCK

In the final days of preproduction, buy twenty percent less negative stock than your projected total. In most locations (and especially in New York City and Los Angeles), you can easily pick up more film or have it delivered to you during the shoot, if and when the occasion arrives.

Because film stock is such a large component of a small budget, being a thrifty shopper is crucial. When it comes to **brand**, you currently have only three choices: *Kodak, Fuji* and, for black and white, *Ilford*. Kodak, the most popular brand, is usually the most expensive, but the difference is slight.

Film stock is rated by **speed**. The faster the speed (signified by a larger number), the less light you'll need. However, you do run into extra grain. Film speed standards are continuously being improved upon, thus increasing your latitudes for lighting. Your cinematographer will have a preference, depending on the circumstances of your shoot.

Stock is sold in rolls of various **lengths**. The standard size rolls are 400 feet and 1,000 feet, but shorter lengths are available for special needs. Not all cameras can accommodate 1,000-foot rolls. And, if you'll be shooting with a hand-held or an especially mobile camera, your camera operator won't want to be weighed down by a heavy roll of film.

Regardless of brand, speed or roll length, you will have opportunities to shop for bargains. The first thing to know is that nobody pays retail for raw stock.

Wholesale

The most common, convenient and safest method is buying negative stock directly from wholesalers. Most will ship film anywhere in the world.

Eastman Kodak has offices in Los Angeles and New York City, as well as in Chicago, Atlanta and Dallas. **Studio Film & Tape** is the national distributor for Fuji; they also sell Kodak (new and gray market), Ilford, and audio, video and still stock. They have offices in New York City, Los Angeles and Chicago. **Steadi Systems** distributes all film formats. They have offices in L.A. and New York City. Currently, these are the biggest companies, but there are other raw stock distributors (most are located in L.A. or N.Y.). Some of these lesser-known distributors may offer wholesale film for less than their better-known competitors.

Ignore quoted rates. Since you're making a large buy, you should be able to get at least a twenty percent discount off wholesale quotes. If a distributor won't negotiate, remind him of the other suppliers you can call.

You should know that stock companies almost always offer a discount to film students; sometimes this is an additional twenty percent. Maybe you or someone in your crew actually is in college. If not, people have been known to create fake student identification cards (the cost of making one is tiny when compared to the amount it can potentially save a person); Kevin Smith of *Clerks* fame is among those who boast openly of this tactic.

Gray Market
The gray market has been around since the "Poverty Row" days of Monogram Pictures. Monogram used to shoot its cheapest B-movies (mostly serials and westerns) for $36,000 in seven days using the film scraps left over from the larger Hollywood studios. They bought these short ends for one-third of the wholesale price (in 1931, this meant one cent per foot instead of three cents).

The gray market is made up of previously bought cans, re-cans and short ends. **Previously bought cans** are those which were purchased but never opened. **Re-cans** were opened and put in a camera magazine but the film was never exposed. **Short ends** are the unexposed ends of exposed film rolls. You can save at least fifty percent by buying gray market stock. Re-cans and short ends are generally cheaper than previously bought cans.

There are businesses in Los Angeles and New York City that specialize in purchasing unused, excess film stock from productions and reselling it to low-budget filmmakers like you. Although these legitimate enterprises test a portion of each roll, you're still taking a chance that picture quality will be noticeably different from roll to roll. Match emulsion numbers, but understand that even this is no guarantee.

In addition, short ends are a hassle, especially if they're less than 100 feet, because you're never sure when they'll run out and you're always changing them. Prices go down the shorter a roll is, but working to squeeze long takes onto small rolls of films will tax your patience.

Sometimes gray market film stock is sold or given away by productions with excess stock. Occasionally, there are ads in industry papers for such film. Better yet, ask around. Free leftovers could be out there for the taking if you approach the right person. If you can get stock for nothing or next-to-nothing, go for it, but you should still get it tested (shoot and develop portions) before production begins.

Let's say you get some free short ends, even though you plan on shooting primarily with negative stock purchased wholesale. Don't use the short ends for reaction shots: subtle color differences between the short ends and the purchased stock may be noticeable. Try to use the short ends for establishing shots or other scenes that stand by themselves so color contrasts are less apparent.

Be careful with shorts, re-cans and previously bought film, but know that they are a valid option for saving money. Also know that, once you've wrapped, the gray market is a way to get cash back for any leftover film stock you may have.

Black Market

This is essentially stolen film, though the sellers will probably try to pass it off as something else. Hot stock will go for at least sixty percent less than wholesale. In addition to morality, quality is a concern. Can you really trust the seller? Buy and shoot at your own risk.

This is a good place for a warning: Keep close track of your production's stock. Store most of it at the producer's home in a cool, dark closet. Only bring in a few more cans than will be needed each day. And when you release stock to the camera assistants, make a careful note of how many cans you turn over and what the serial numbers are.

Sound Tape Stock

In relation to film, 1/4-inch sound tape stock is a minor expense, costing less than one-tenth as much as film stock. Even digital audio tape (DAT) is not a big expense. Sound stock is available from sound houses and from many of the same wholesalers that sell raw film stock. Popular brands include Maxell, TDK, and Ampex. Either the production will purchase this for the sound mixer or the mixer will buy it and bill the production.

11/STUFF

When you get ready for production, what stuff you don't already own, you'll have to buy, rent, borrow, make, substitute for or do without. By all means, before pulling out your production checkbook, make sure your family, friends, cast or crew (or the family and friends of your cast and crew) don't already have the thingamajig, or maybe one of them knows how you can obtain it for little or no money. Don't be bashful; asking around can save a lot of money. Next, get ready to barter.

CAMERA PACKAGE

Rates for cameras are negotiated as part of a broader **"camera package."** In addition to the camera, this usually includes such items as lenses, filters, a video assist monitor, cables, magazines, a tripod and all necessary cases. Camera houses have rate cards that list their daily rental prices. What you should try to do is rent the package from them for a "two-day week" or a "three-day week." In other words, you'll pay for two or three days but keep the camera for seven. "Four-day weeks" are fairly standard in the industry and getting people to a "three-day" is within reach. You'll have to haggle hard to get a "two-day." But set your sights high. By the way, weekends, when cameras are least used, are almost always billed as "one-day," meaning, you can pick up the gear on Friday evening and return it on Monday morning—you'll get two and a half days for the price of one. This is a principal reason why some films shoot only on weekends (see "SCHEDULE: Breakdown & Shooting Schedule").

Panavision and *Arriflex* 35mm camera packages rent for $1,500 to $2,000 per day, or $4,500 to $6,000 for a "three-day week." Their 16mm and Super 16 cousins are approximately half as much to lease. Generally, *Eclair, Bolex, Mitchell* and other brands are cheaper to rent—sometimes a lot cheaper. The various items in your camera package will influence its price. **Video assist** (a monitor which shows approximately what the lens sees) is usually extra. You'll need at least two **magazines** (the more the better) for every speed of film stock you use so that one magazine can be loaded while you're shooting with the other.

The number and types of **lenses** you rent will also influence the package price, sometimes to a great extent. Lenses are identified by their focal lengths (expressed in millimeters). And, special lenses, such as telephoto, wide angle and snorkel, can be expensive. In addition to valid aesthetic uses, a **zoom lens** (the "poor man's dolly") will allow those of you on a tight budget to simulate forward and backward tracking shots as well as change from, say, a medium shot to a close-up without investing time to block a dolly movement or create a new setup. A wide variety of **filters** (polarizing, fog, diffusing, etc.) will also influence price. The director and cinematographer should determine their lens and filter needs early in order to incorporate them into the budget and the shooting script.

When renting cameras and lighting/grip packages, avoid businesses with anything less than a stellar reputation—even if they offer a tremendous bargain. Delays caused by faulty equipment can easily cost several times as much as your savings on the initial rental deal. Your cinematographer should know the reputations of local renters. D.p.'s also may have established working relationships with certain equipment houses and this can save you considerably.

Sometimes 16mm and, less commonly, Super 16 camera packages can be rented cheaply from individuals. Some cinematographers may own their cameras (like sound mixers, you'll probably have to pay them an additional equipment rental fee). However, do not get suckered into a bargain that doesn't meet your needs. A mediocre d.p. who owns an outdated Bolex is no bargain. Quality is paramount.

Wherever you get your camera, have your cinematographer test it in order to detect any problems early. Watch for light leaks and scratches on the prime lenses. You may want to run a small amount of film through and have it developed. Any blurring will mean the shutter is out of synchronization. Focus problems may be caused by the pressure plate. These must be fixed by an expert before the first day of shooting. During production, the camera rental house may not have a replacement available and any quick fix may not be quick enough.

If your budget can handle it, having a **second camera** available for your entire shoot will be a welcome addition. Shooting simultaneously from two angles can be especially effective when capturing complex action or fight scenes. But even if you can't squeeze a high-quality second camera into your budget, there are cheap, **"wild"** (unable to be synced with sound) or **"blimped"** (noisy unless soundproofed) cameras that can be used for MOS (without sound) shots. And it may be worth it to rent an additional camera for a day or two and have a small second unit crew (perhaps just a camera operator and a grip) pick up establishing shots, inserts, etc., while the first unit is filming the main action and dialogue. The money spent on the second camera may be much easier on your budget than extending the production schedule to get the same shots with first unit.

Finally, a camera is perhaps the single most important and expensive item in your shoot. Treat it with special care and respect. The director, the camera assistants and the cinematographer should be the <u>only ones</u> to touch the camera. It should go home with one of you (probably the 1st a.c.) at the end of each day's shoot. Never leave it overnight on a set or in a truck.

DOLLY

You don't have to have a real camera dolly. Micro-budget films are sometimes shot with a hand-held camera (as was Nick Gomez's *Laws of Gravity* [1992]) or with a makeshift "dolly" (*El Mariachi* used a wheelchair—a common substitute). For that matter, nothing says you have to move the camera at all (as in the static shots of *Stranger Than Paradise*).

The lack of smooth, formal dolly movements are sometimes turned into an advantage by independent filmmakers. Hand-held shots can create a documentary quality; static shots, often held a little "too long," can give a laid-back, ironic feel; and quick-cut editing can disguise the scarcity of camera moves and produce a frenetic pace.

Still, if you want to move the camera forward and backward, left and right, up and down, the most efficient method is with an actual dolly. But, they're not cheap. Rental prices range between $700 to $1,500 per week, depending on size. And if you're dollying outside or on uneven flooring, you may need tracks (an extra cost). In Los Angeles, there are houses that specialize in renting only dollies and cranes; elsewhere, you'll probably rent from a standard camera or grip house.

A dolly is generally considered a necessary filmmaking expense. If you can't fit one into your budget but you want tracking shots, a **wheelchair** can be rented or bought cheaply from any medical supply house. Make sure it moves smoothly and without noise. The d.p. sits like a patient and aims the camera; the dolly grip pushes like a nurse.

Also know that sheets of plywood can make rough surfaces smooth. To fill in floor, street and sidewalk cracks, use extremely fine aquarium sand or sugar.

LIGHTING/GRIP PACKAGE

Photo floods, halogens, fluorescents, tripods, fresnels, arcs, reflectors, scrims, barn doors, sandbags, silks, cables, flags, clamps, ladders, apple boxes, tarps . . . whew, there's a lot of stuff you'll need. As a result, the lighting/grip package will be a major budget component.

Again, shop around. As with cameras, lighting rental houses should give you at least a four-day week but try for a two-day week. Prices are somewhat dependent on the production season and how busy the rental house is. Don't rent things you know you won't need but do cover all realistic possibilities up-front. You don't want to return later to pick up items individually, as this can bleed a budget fast.

Production companies sometimes have equipment sitting around, unused, that they will rent cheaply or lend for free—if only somebody trustworthy would inquire. Be prepared to leave a substantial deposit wherever you borrow.

For those of you on a micro-budget, equipment can be improvised, gathered from the closets of your crew, or purchased cheaply at your neighborhood hardware store. A bounce board can be a square of styrofoam; a standing reflector (to reflect light) can be polished sheet metal; a flag (to block light) can be a piece of felt stretched over an old picture frame or a piece of cardboard; aluminum foil and squares of old window screen can be small reflectors and scrims (to strengthen or weaken light).

In an extreme cash crunch, lighting can be accomplished cheaply (but not ideally) with available "practical" sources (make sure bulbs are at least 250 watts), a single keylight to remove the shadows from faces and high-speed film stock. Rodriguez lit *El Mariachi*'s interiors with only a few 250-watt bulbs and improvised reflectors. The results were pallid and flat, but the film was released to theaters by a major Hollywood studio. So, you never know. This method, however, would be a last resort for the truly poverty-stricken. (See "MAKING A MOVIE: Speed" for the basics of lighting.)

In the world of independent filmmaking, some grips, gaffers and cinematographers have their own trucks and equipment. If you use their wheels and gear, they'll come on-board as part of an overall package deal, serving as your key grip or gaffer or cinematographer. This may save you considerable dough, but be careful that the equipment owner has everything you need and that it is in good, working condition. Most importantly, make sure that the truck, equipment and the person are perfect for you . . . it will be hard to fire an incompetent boob if that person will be driving off with the equipment you need for your shoot.

TRUCK & GENERATOR

To get your equipment to the location or set, you'll need at least one **large truck with locks**. If you'll be shooting at only one or two secure spots, you may be able to unload and store all your gear in a room there and rent the truck just for moving in and out. Otherwise, the truck will serve as your equipment room and will never be completely unloaded. You'll rent a truck (or two or three, depending on your equipment) for your entire shoot (not an insignificant expense). And, you'll need to find a secure spot very near your location where you can park it while shooting and an even more secure place where you can leave it overnight. Additionally, you may need a driver (or two or three). As mentioned under "lighting/

grip package," the truck and equipment sometimes come together, joined by a mandatory crew person.

Depending on your ability or inability to tie in to power sources at your location(s), you'll probably need to rent a **generator**. Get a nearly silent gas unit, capable of meeting all electrical requirements. The more powerful your lights, the bigger the "genny" you'll need. Make sure somebody on your crew (perhaps in the electrical department) is expert at operating it.

SOUND EQUIPMENT
As stated earlier, the sound mixer usually has his own gear, which he will rent to you. He should have the following equipment:

- either a Nagra 1/4-inch tape recorder or a digital tape (DAT) recorder;

- a modern mixing board with enough channels to cover every speaking actor in your biggest scene;

- all necessary microphones, cables and headphones.

If he doesn't own his equipment (or if he doesn't own the <u>right</u> equipment), items can be rented from a sound house, as well as from many camera and grip establishments. As for other gear, try to negotiate for less than a "four-day week." Also, some appliance and department stores have a thirty day return policy. Some people have been known to buy an expensive DAT machine, try it out on a film set for four weeks, and then, on the twenty-ninth day, having decided it's just not quite right, return it for a full refund.

EXPENDABLES
Expendables include such items as lighting gels, filters, bulbs, multicolored tape, batteries, etc. In other words, disposable but necessary production items. They're not all cheap, and you may need to buy large quantities of them. Some are available only from specific rental houses; others can be purchased at half that price at your local hardware or discount department store.

Long before production begins, stock up on such common items as aluminum foil, batteries and tape (you'll need a variety of colored tape to lay down marks).

Keep careful records of expendable purchases. Make sure your crew members are not overcharging you for inexpensive, store-bought items and that they're not taking any extras home. Also, remember that you can resell your own unused items to houses or production companies after your shoot.

ART DEPARTMENT/SET CONSTRUCTION
This category is a big question mark. If you need to build and dress sets, you can easily spend more than $40,000 here. On the other hand, a location shoot might not spend a dime on design. Your production designer should be an expert at making do with what's available and finding bargains for what's not. Those in charge of the film's look must not be strangers to thrift stores and salvage centers.

Flats (fake walls) and lumber often can be borrowed from other productions or scrounged from almost anywhere. Paint is usually on sale at a hardware store. Posters and the like can be obtained for free from a few hundred government and private agencies. Furniture and decorative items are sold at garage sales, thrift stores and through your local Salvation Army. Don't overlook the fact that many items can be borrowed. Label every item and make sure all of them are returned—undamaged. With planning and ingenuity, your production design bills can be kept in check.

PROPS
It may seem like "anything and everything," from any time in history and from any place in the world, is available at prop rental houses or studio departments. But anything and everything will cost you dearly. As with art and set construction items, props can be purchased at discount stores, yard sales and thrift shops. These items also can be borrowed. Begin collecting necessary props early, when you'll have time to hunt for bargains.

Dangerous items (like blank-shooting guns) or true exotica (like medieval torture devices) will probably need to be rented from an official prop house. But, most other items can be found for less elsewhere.

An ordinary rental establishment will often have what you're looking for at a lower rate than an industry shop. Also, some non-rental businesses may let you borrow certain otherwise expensive items in exchange for an acknowledgement (free advertising) in your end credits. Again, the chances of this happening for little or no money are greatest outside of New York City and Los Angeles (the "prop" section of L.A. industry directories are filled with non-rental, non-industry places eager to lend their wares to productions . . . for a fee).

When it comes to crucial props, it's best to have most smaller items in duplicate or triplicate, in case one breaks or disappears. And don't forget that if the item has to be broken on-screen, you'll need several identical copies for multiple takes.

WARDROBE

As mentioned earlier, micro-budget films often don't have costumes, per se; the cast members wear what they own. If this is the case, make certain in the rehearsal stage that all actors have enough appropriate clothing and jewelry. If they don't, make sure they do before production begins. Approve every item at least two weeks before it is to appear on-screen.

Plan ahead and you can avoid spending a lot on wardrobe. If clothes need to be purchased, they can often be found at thrift shops, discount stores or flea markets. And this, like the "No Questions Asked" return policy for some electronic equipment and props, is a category in which people have been known to "buy" an item, wear it on-screen, and then return it for a refund. As with props, your clothing items may require multiples. This is especially true when something needs to be ripped, bled on or otherwise soiled on-screen.

Historical or exotic costumes and a variety of official-looking uniforms can be created from scratch or rented from costume shops in larger metropolitan areas. Avoid the generic Halloween look. Also know that there are laws against just any citizen wearing authentic military or police uniforms; you'll probably need to submit a written request to your permit office, stating that official-looking uniforms will be used only in an innocent film production and not in a bank heist. Do this early to allow time for the request to be processed.

MISCELLANEOUS

What else? Probably a lot of seemingly insignificant budget-nibblers that somehow will conspire to take a big bite when you're not looking. Makeup; hair supplies; at least one first-aid kit near the set at all times; fire extinguishers; walkie-talkies so crew members can communicate through walls, windows and diverse locations;

megaphones; tables; chairs; garbage cans; flashlights; traffic cones; umbrellas and canopies; sound blankets; cellular phones . . . .And just when you think you've covered everything, new needs will suddenly materialize. Office supplies; cleaning supplies; unforeseen supplies. Then you'll turn around and equipment will break; gear will disappear.

Try to set aside at least $1,000 in your budget for **miscellaneous expenses** and **missing and damaged**. And the producer or unit production manager needs to keep a tight fist on the petty cash. Hope for the best and prepare for the worst.

12/LAB, PART 1

By having all of your production and post-production needs handled by the same laboratory, you probably will save money and receive more consistent service. For now, though, let's focus only on production lab work.

First, let's assume that you'll be editing on a nonlinear system. You'll need to have your negative film developed and transferred to videotape each day. This process called **telecine** will be a large, unavoidable expense (perhaps your largest). The videotape can be in any size, depending on the capabilities of your nonlinear editing system (Beta SP is the highest quality videotape, 3/4" next and VHS is the lowest quality). The lab should supply you with additional VHS copies of your dailies so you can easily monitor what you've shot and how it's being processed. The lab may also print a small amount of film (perhaps 400 feet) for you to screen. Simultaneously, your production sound will need to be transferred from tape to videotape and synced with the picture. This can be done at a sound lab but most film facilities also perform this service and it's easier if everything is handled under the same roof.

As with camera and equipment rental, don't agree to the terms of a house's rate card. You should be able to negotiate a cost that is ten percent to forty percent less than any printed rate. This may be a good time to pull out a student identification card. Shop around but go only with a respected and established laboratory. Your film might be the largest material investment you control in your life; do not hand it over to just any cheap darkroom.

In the Los Angeles area, the lab of choice for independent filmmakers is **Foto-Kem/Foto-Tronics** in Burbank. There are economical alternatives but Foto-Kem has competitive rates and a great reputation in the indie community. Other good facilities include CFI, Filmservice and DeLuxe Laboratories.

In New York City, **DuArt** is *the* name for independents (as well as for most studio films that shoot in the area). There are other places, but no lab has a reputation as stellar as DuArt's. And they give special care to indies, sometimes even working on a deferred-pay basis. Also know that DuArt perfected the optical printing equipment necessary for film blow-ups, and they handle more doubling of 16mm or Super 16 film than any other lab on the planet.

In the rest of the country, your laboratory options may be limited. You can always go the (often expensive) route of shipping or driving negative film to L.A. or N.Y.C. If this is not an option, try to find a local place with significant experience in your format and length. In many areas, labs handle mostly 16mm industrial or educational reels. These businesses may not have the equipment or expertise to develop Super 16 or 35mm film and if they do, processing thousands of feet of film quickly each night over a month's time may be too difficult for them to perform to your satisfaction. If you have any doubts about a laboratory, have it print 100 feet of film in your format. (In an attempt to win your business, they should do this for free.)

Buyer beware: you may be a rookie yourself but do not trust your dream film to a rookie lab. Go only with a respected and eminently competent facility.

13/PUBLICITY, PART 1

Studio films and large independents hire a **unit publicist** to attract attention before and during the shoot. Unless you have a budget higher than $1 million, such a crew member may be an unaffordable luxury, at which point, this role will most probably be absorbed by you, all other above-the-line people, your mom, your best friend and anyone else who can spread the word.

SPREADING THE WORD, PART 1

Now and forever, the more people who know about your film, the better. Along with the scattershot approach of telling everyone you know, you'll want to target acquisition executives at independent film distribution companies; these are the people who buy. They may learn about your production through the grapevine and contact you, or you can contact them yourself. At this point, simply let them know that you exist and that you're making a movie they absolutely will not want to miss when it's completed. Whet their appetites by describing your feature in three compelling lines or less.

Until your film is sold (and maybe not even then), never disclose your budget. Give this same caveat to everyone working with you on this project. This is very important! Distributors will assume that you're broke or indebted and that you're looking to recoup fast; if they know your movie cost $100,000, they may try to tempt you with $110,000. But if they're not sure if you spent $100,000 or $300,000, you have an advantage. When people ask about your budget you need only say, "Less than a million." (If your budget is

$500,000, say, "Less than two million." If your budget is $1 million to $4 million, say, "Less than ten million.")

One of the first things you should do to spread the word is get your film into the "trades," the entertainment industry newspapers. You can list your film—right next to the studio blockbusters—in the production charts of *Daily Variety, Weekly Variety* and *The Hollywood Reporter.* A few months before production, call them; they'll fax you a form to fill out and fax back. Then, they'll print your listing in the "Development," "Films in Preparation" or "Preproduction" category (new entries are boxed when they first appear in the paper); they'll switch you to "Production" when you reach your start date. The listing includes your film's title, genre, a contact address and phone number and the names of the principal cast and crew members.

Besides the trades, there are a plethora of other places to get preproduction and production coverage for your film. Magazines and newspapers, even local television newscasts and radio shows, often realize that the trials and tribulations of low-budget filmmakers create fascinating human interest stories.

(Almost) any publicity is good publicity. At this stage, local publicity could bring more money from investors or free services and products from businesses. Someone may want to shoot a "Making of" film or video. Let him. The Internet, school papers, church bulletins—these are all viable sources of publicity. If you have a story and you're willing to push it, you can generate a lot of coverage before filming begins.

It may not entice distributors to call, but even a small, indie film should consider having **clothing** (T-shirts, hats, sweatshirts, jackets) printed with its title and perhaps some other distinguishing logo. (Hats are the cheapest item to make but T-shirts are a close second, and more people will probably wear a shirt.) Try to get a cut-rate deal from a silk-screener in exchange for a "thank you" in the credits. During preproduction and production, the main function of movie clothing is to foster a united spirit among your cast and crew. Shirts serve as uniforms, and uniforms throughout the ages— be they for soldiers, sports teams or the Girl Scouts—have helped to imbibe people with a sense of shared purpose. Giving free clothes to your cast and crew is a relatively minor investment that can pay off in lots of enthusiasm, pride and team spirit. Also, because everyone wearing the threads is a walking billboard, shirts and hats help to legitimize your movie. After the shoot wraps, movie clothes serve as advertisements at film festivals and among the general public. Distributors routinely print all kinds of clothing to spread the word.

STILLS

Production stills are of paramount importance in generating publicity. Try to hire an experienced **still photographer**. This person won't need to be on-set (or paid) for every day of your shoot. But, make sure he's around when you're shooting the most interesting stuff. And, of course, he should take high-quality shots of all your principal actors. In addition to photos of the movie and performers, be certain there are plenty of shots of the director and, to a lesser degree, the producer(s) and cinematographer. (Much of the publicity in the world of film festivals and independents centers around the filmmaker[s]. This is especially true of micro-budget fare, which seldom feature name actors.)

If you cannot find the money in your budget for a professional photographer or you cannot find someone to work for a few days for deferred pay (and credit and meals), assign someone from your crew (or your family) to assume the photo-snapping responsibilities; make sure he uses a good 35mm camera.

Negotiate the lowest possible processing fees at a top-flight photo lab. Contact sheets are less expensive than slides; negative strips are even cheaper, but they're very difficult to discern. Under most circumstances, you will probably need at least twice as many black-and-white stills as color.

FREE STUFF

You can gain publicity by giving it away. During preproduction, look through your script for potential brand name items (food, beer, clothes, etc.) that could appear on-screen. Write or call the appropriate companies; don't overlook local businesses. In a potential blockbuster, companies sometimes pay studios big money for product placement—sums that may exceed your entire budget! Unfortunately, knowing the odds are stacked against a huge audience ever seeing your little movie, such corporations probably aren't going to pay you anything for "integrated advertising."

If a company won't pay for product placement in your film, it may provide you with free products in exchange for your giving them exposure in your soon-to-be-hip independent feature. Request more than you'll need because they'll probably give you less than you want. Like so much in independent filmmaking, it never hurts to ask.

In order to show any name brand product on-screen, you'll need a signed release form from the company's legal department; when arranging for this release, it might be an ideal time to inquire about free products. Corporations often want to read a script and/or receive written assurance that their product won't be shown in a negative light.

Finally, whether or not their product or business name appears on-screen, local businesses may provide free or discounted items or services in exchange for a "thank you" in the end credits. The further you are from L.A. and N.Y.C., the more people want to help. Remember: the general public thinks filmmaking is "glamorous."

14/PREPRODUCTION GUT CHECK

"Before a picture, the best thing to do is go to the gym and spend two months just working out . . . because making a picture is an endurance contest with yourself."

— *Steven Spielberg*

You can still pull out. You can still turn back. You probably have invested a lot of time, but most of the money is still in the bank, waiting to be spent. Worries are nearly inevitable, but if you have strong, lingering doubts—if you can't shake the feeling that the script is missing something or you've cast the wrong person in a crucial role or you and the cinematographer are not seeing eye to eye, you can still pull the plug. You can still push the start date back. You can still give it all up and sell tube socks.

But once you shout, "Action!" and film starts moving through the camera, there's no stopping this movie train without suffering a terrible crash. From Day One, a film production devours money like an insatiable monster. After one week of filming, even if you wanted to, it wouldn't make sense to halt production—more than half of your budget will be gone or contractually tied up.

If you're not pulling out, then push forward with everything you've got. It's natural to be worried sick, but if you still believe in your vision, then never let on to the cast and crew that you're troubled. Wear a smile through the most nerve-racking situations. And put every ounce of energy you have into this movie because it may be your best (or only) chance to present your vision as a filmmaker.

THE DAY BEFORE

Follow this checklist:

√ Locations and catering are confirmed.

√ The truck is rented.

√ All equipment is picked up and stored at the first location/ stage; or, the truck and gear are kept in a secure place overnight.

√ The camera has been tested.

√ Film and audio stock have been purchased and stored.

√ Rented props, costumes or other items necessary for Day One are picked up.

√ The first set is dressed (if possible).

√ The assistant director confirms that all cast and crew members are aware of call times; which parts of the scrip will be shot; and precise directions to the set.

√ The director and cinematographer review Day One's shot list (and, if necessary, diagrams or storyboards). TIP: Keep the first day's shooting load lighter than the rest because it often takes the crew a day to get into the groove.

√ Try to sleep—you'll need it.

PRODUCTION

15/MAKING A MOVIE

You've called, "Action!" You're rolling. There's no stopping the movie train; it's full speed ahead. Your entire life, for the next few weeks, will be absorbed by photofloods and held together with gaffer's tape. Brutal but, hopefully, still a blast. Enjoy.

A TYPICAL DAY

Every production is different but some procedures are considered "standard." The most basic of these is to keep at least a 10-hour turnaround between the wrap time and the first call of the next day. *Don't mess with this rule.*

So, assuming the previous day wrapped before 9:00 p.m., a typical shooting day might go something like this:

5:45 a.m.   Wake-up. Shower. Commute.

6:45 a.m.   Director, assistant director, cinematographer and producer arrive and review the day's schedule.

7:00 a.m.   First call. A light breakfast is laid out for all. Crew members arrive and begin lighting and dressing the set. Actors go into makeup. (TIP: Actors' calls should be staggered. The earliest calls should be for those actors scheduled to appear on-camera first or for those with any special makeup needs.)

8:00 a.m.   Begin lighting the set, using stand-ins for actors. A stand-in may be a crew person not currently working (i.e., p.a., boom operator, photographer, etc.) or anyone hanging around.

8:30 a.m.	On-set rehearsal for actors, with the camera and sound crews. Lights are tweaked with the actors in place. (TIP: In order to utilize time efficiently, don't wait for actors to come out of makeup in order to get your first shot of the day. If the crew is ready to go, get footage of inserts [close-ups of items] or shoot whatever else you can capture without performers. Because of makeup time, it is best not to schedule master shots with several actors first thing in the morning.)
9:00 a.m.	First shot of the day. Commence filming. You'll go through various setups, experience various crises.
1:00 p.m.	Lunch break. Hot meal.
1:30 p.m.	Back to filming.
7:30 p.m.	Wrap for the day. All equipment is secured and/or packed for the next day. Call sheets are distributed for the next day's schedule; anyone who didn't receive a call sheet should be telephoned.
	(OR: If you're not stopping, 7:30 p.m. is the time to break for dinner. Thirty minutes later, get back to filming. Try to wrap before midnight.)
8:00 p.m.	Camera assistants file camera reports; script supervisor completes notes; director, assistant director, cinematographer and producer review the day's work and discuss the next day's strategy.
8:30 p.m.	Truck and camera are secured for the night. Someone trustworthy (probably the 2nd a.c.) delivers the film and sound rolls to the lab.
9:30 p.m.	Return home. Eat, if necessary. Set alarm for 5:45 a.m. Dream big.

PRODUCING

During preproduction, producing was mostly about finding the money and planning how to spend it. During production, it's time to do the spending. At this point, the principal responsibility of the producer(s) and staff (especially the production manager) is to oversee the movie's business transactions. Such affairs will include catering; transportation; managing locations and stages; procuring raw stock and equipment; acting as liaison with the lab; overseeing publicity matters; and paying the cast, crew and various vendors. You should not try to be both director and producer during the production, even if your credits read this way; give the checkbook to the u.p.m.

It is also the producer's responsibility to make sure any production problems are resolved (see "SAVING A MOVIE"). These often messy matters are handled by the producer so the director can concentrate solely on the film's creative aspects. The producer has artistic input, too, but when the camera is rolling, it's more important that he keep a tight hold on the money, paperwork and itinerary—all the while remaining focused on completing the film on-schedule and on-budget.

ASSISTANT DIRECTING

On an independent film, the role of the assistant director is more important than ever. Yes, the cast and crew will probably be smaller than on a studio shoot, but the a.d. on an indie will also have less assistance. The assistant director is the "calvary colonel," so to speak: ever vigilant on the battlefield, obediently following strategic orders from above and routinely leading the charging troops forward. Therefore, your a.d. must be hard-working, even-tempered and well-respected. It is the assistant director who makes sure the camera and sound crews are ready and he's the one who says, "Quiet on the set!" and "We're rolling!" It is the a.d.'s responsibility to see that the director stays on the shooting schedule and that all crew members are performing their jobs efficiently. It is crucial for any motion picture to come in on-time and on-budget, but it is especially so when the production cannot afford to lose one hour or one dollar.

The a.d. maintains a **production report**, listing all the activity (number of setups, length of time for setups, amount of film consumed, break times, etc.) of each shooting day. This essential data is available to the producer or director to review at any time in order to assess progress. If your film is SAG, the a.d. also will be responsible for filling out actors' Exhibit G forms.

Another duty of the assistant director (usually a 2nd a.d.) is to prepare the **call sheets**. These will contain such information as the location(s) of the shoot (often with maps), which actors are needed, the call time for each member of the cast and crew and any special circumstances for that day. Even the smallest productions should use call sheets. A computer creates such paperwork with ease, but you can also hand-write the information on pre-printed forms and then photocopy them. Call sheets are distributed at the end of each day. If times are changed or if some cast or crew members left early and did not receive a call sheet, the a.d. will need to phone them with an update.

CONTINUITY

Continuity is the internal logic of shots so they match when strung together. Of course, they are not strung together until the film is edited, and therein lies the challenge. Motion pictures are almost always shot out of sequence. Most times, the continuous shots seen on screen are actually filmed days or weeks apart. Proper planning as well as copious notes and dedicated vigilance are imperative in order to make what may look like a mishmash of footage now seem perfectly logical later.

Proper continuity includes:

- Obeying the laws of the **center line** (an imaginary line between two characters or growing out in both directions from one character). The camera should stay on one side of the center line unless we clearly see the line broken and reestablished. Otherwise, characters will appear to unnaturally jump from one side of the frame to the other.

- The matching of **eyelines**. If two people are gazing at each other, one must look to the left side of the camera while the other must look to the right side of the camera (and to the same degree).

- **Direction of movement** across the frame. If a car travels through a shot from left to right, the car chasing it must also travel from left to right or the autos will appear (incorrectly) to be traveling towards each other.

- A logical **progression of time**. For example, clocks and watches should be in sync from scene to scene; burning cigarettes should slowly turn to ash (and not be various lengths in various shots). Sometimes, items may undergo large leaps (i.e., meals can disappear, clocks can jump hours ahead) to show a progression of time but this, too, must happen logically.

- A consistent **placement of actors and props.** People and items must not seem to jump around a room, remain still when they're supposed to be moving, disappear for no reason or magically reappear when they should be gone.

- **Costumes** (even little things like buttons and the placement of collars), **hair styles** and **makeup** should not change within a scene without provocation. Blown-up on a big screen, what seems insignificant during production can become laughable later.

- **Lighting** must be consistent between shots of the same subject(s), even if the shots are taken from various lengths or angles. The cinematographer and his crew must make special note of this. Exteriors can be especially difficult on partly cloudy days and as the sun travels across the sky.

- **Point-of-view** footage must be properly set up by the previous shot(s); and, you must make sure you shoot the previous shot(s). For example, if we're seeing things from someone's perspective, in most situations we must know whose perspective this is; this should not change without us being told visually.

- **Acting consistency.** Dialogue, actions and emotions should match throughout or they should alter at an acceptable pace.

There are times when rules of continuity can be broken, as in a **montage** (an assortment of shots which, together, tell their own story), when the film wants to show a progression of time or to exhibit a particular stylistic effect. But for the most part, continuity standards should be closely adhered to.

The principal tools for maintaining consistency are the script supervisor's **notes** and the **eyes** and **memory** of the director, script supervisor and others in the cast and crew. Another useful device is **Polaroid snapshots.** Budget for a Polaroid camera and film (not inexpensive). Assign someone to snap photos of prop placement, set decorations, makeup effects, lighting—anything that needs to remain the same. Undoubtedly, items will be moved in order to set lights and equipment. If Polaroids are taken before items are moved, things can be returned to their same positions when the camera begins shooting again.

Additionally, if you're using **video assist**, plugging a **VCR** into the monitor can aid with continuity and reduce your Polaroid bill. Turn the video camera on before each take and off afterwards. (With cheaper systems, the recorded version will flicker because film is shot at a different speed than video.) **Video dailies** also provide help but they're less immediate: you won't get Monday's footage till Tuesday.

Rehearsals and **master shots** also aid in the maintenance of uniformity by providing a clear idea of where things and people should be as you move in for closer coverage. The entire crew should watch full-scene rehearsals and master shots in order to help preserve visual harmony when the camera rolls.

Continuity will primarily be the responsibility of the script supervisor and the director. But the art department (especially the prop master) can lend assistance, and everyone —actors, makeup artist, cinematographer, etc.—should try to keep things consistent.

A final note: Never think the little things won't matter. Everything will be magnified many times on the big screen and everything can be paused and studied in perpetuity on small screens.

SPEED

The saying, "Time is money," is never more true than when making a motion picture. Spend too much time on one setup and you'll have to rush through or scrap several others (sacrificing quality) or extend your shooting schedule (sacrificing money).

Good directing is good planning, and good planning conserves time. You should have a strategy of attack every step of the way, especially when working with a meager budget. During preproduction, you prepared the shooting script, shot lists, diagrams of sets and locations and perhaps storyboards (see "SCHEDULE: shooting strategy"). Now, during production, you review each day's setups with the cinematographer and assistant director; update as necessary. Plan all shots to best utilize every minute.

Knowing how many setups you plan to shoot in each direction is important, so you'll only need to "turn the room around" (move the lights and equipment from one side of the set to the other—a huge time-eater) once per day per set. If possible, film a simple setup in one area while much of the crew is preparing for a more complex setup in another. To get things done at a brisk pace, you'll need a proficient crew capable of knocking off twenty-five or more setups each day.

Unfortunately, when working with a limited budget, with a small crew and on a tight schedule, money will sometimes affect shot selection. If a setup is taking too long or a particular shot isn't clicking, you have to be flexible enough to change your plan and cover the same material in an easier, more efficient manner (see "SAVING A MOVIE: schedule problems").

Setting lights usually consumes the most time. Therefore, what follows is a very quick lesson in **lighting basics**. The three principal categories are:

- **key** (the main light illuminating a subject);

- **back** (gives depth and creates a halo effect between the subject and the background);

- **fill** (diminishes shadows around the subject).

Things can get complicated. There are many types of lights and bulbs, many accessories available to create shadows and reflections and alter colors, etc., but key, back and fill are the basics.

It's best to do one general setup (key/back/fill) for a scene, then add and subtract lights and accessories as the coverage changes. To save time, you might need to start shooting before things are "tweaked" (altered in small ways) to their maximum potential. The cinematographer and gaffer should be aware of the schedule and what they can and cannot do in the time allotted. The assistant director needs to eye his watch like a hawk. The director always makes the final call when caught between the lights (d.p.) and the clock (a.d.). It's a trade-off, but realize that taking precious time to perfectly illuminate a subject may cause you to rush through other shots (or scratch them entirely), thus hurting your film's quality in the long run.

On the set, rehearse with the actors while the crew is setting up. Make sure the cast members know their lines and **marks** (where they are to be on the set, usually "marked" with tape that is not seen on screen). Don't over-rehearse, especially when it comes to emotional sequences; situations can lose their immediacy quickly when rehearsed too often. Rehearsals (at least walk-throughs) will also be necessary for the crew to properly perform dolly shots or

125

complex focusing, and for the sound mixer's placement of microphones and setting of channel levels. Practice until all principals involved—actors, cinematographer, sound mixer and you—are totally satisfied. The time and money it takes to rehearse is minimal compared to the dollars expended once film is rolling. And, things always go faster and more smoothly when people know what they're doing.

To maintain a brisk pace, you'll need everyone working together as a team; and, a team works best when the morale is high. Good food, comfortable conditions, adequate sleep and words of encouragement are paramount to keeping your cast and crew working as hard on the sixteenth day as on the second. Marshaling the crew will primarily be the job of the director, assistant director and cinematographer; the producer (from a perspective away from the set) should concentrate on keeping everyone on schedule.

SOUND

Many inexperienced directors give little attention to sound until post-production. DO NOT MAKE THIS MISTAKE! Before the first take from a new setup, allow time for the proper placement of microphones, for rehearsals with the boom microphone operator, sound checks and for the possible dampening of outside noise. While shooting exteriors, the microphones may need to be sheltered with an in-line filter or wind screen (low-budget alternative: a nylon stocking). Do not roll film until cars, planes, people or any other outside noises pass.

During production, the mixer should record room tone, sound effects and wild lines. **Room tones** (the ambient background hum) will be used during the sound editing phase to fill in dead spots and to hide imperfections. **Production sound effects** can be anything and everything. Although virtually all effects can be found or made in post, it's cheaper and usually more realistic if they are recorded on location. You may not use them later, but at least you will have the option. **Wild lines** are dialogue segments recorded without the camera that did not come out well in the original sync recording or that occur in **voice-over** (with the speaker off-screen). These can also be done in post, but you can save time and money by recording them now.

By the way, everything about sound so far has assumed that you'll record in sync on location. You don't have to. Micro-budget movies, including *Breathless* and *El Mariachi*, have been shot MOS, as are many studio efforts throughout the world (most notably in Spain and Hong Kong). In such an effort, the audio is recorded wild and dubbed in later. This allows you to save money on a sound crew, but, more importantly, it enables you to conserve a huge amount of time (and money) by not fretting about line readings while rolling film. The problem with this method is that the audio is usually horrible. If you know the native tongues of either *Breathless* (French) or *El Mariachi* (Spanish), you'll know that the voices never quite match the lips; something seems off. Despite the significant savings of filming MOS, it is strongly recommended that you shoot a "talkie."

SPECIAL EFFECTS & STUNTS

Special effects create a unique challenge for the independent filmmaker. Some can be created with relative ease; others are unthinkable for any movie budgeted at less than $40 million. Here's the line on the most popular FX:

Gunshots are as common in movie theaters as popcorn; the sound of gats blasting away fills even the smallest budgeted films (like *El Mariachi*). Gunfire is a minor expense, but doing it safely is another matter.

Blanks are Hollywood's ammo of choice because they produce a flare and a realistic puff of smoke when shot. But blanks can kill. Lead actor Brandon Lee was mortally wounded on the set of *The Crow* when a cartridge accidentally discharged from a blank-shooting gun. If you must use blanks and a real gun (actually, most movies don't use "real guns," but rather, guns with a smaller barrel so the cartridges, hopefully, don't discharge) hire a munitions expert for those days when guns will be used. This person will load the firearms with blanks (they can also be loaded at the rental place) and set up proper safety standards for their use, including notifying the police. Even with precautions, *it's dangerous to play with guns*.

The truth is, the audio sound of virtually all gunshots is added later, in post-production, because blanks rarely sound the way we expect movie gunshots to sound. Firing a blank is all about the visual, a flare lasting a fraction of a second. For this reason, if the gat will only be going off in a long shot or if it won't be shown firing on screen, use a prop gun that is incapable of shooting anything. If the blast is on screen, you can still fake it in the editing room by inserting one white frame at the moment the gun "fires." In addition, there are prop guns that are incapable of shooting, yet they make a near-realistic flash. Consider these options.

Squibs (small explosives) are used to mimic the effect of bullets connecting. They're usually filled with fake blood and then rigged together in plastic packs, which are then taped to the actor. When they're set off, they explode, making it look like the actor is hit and injured. As with blanks, squibs are a mainstay of low-budget filmmaking. Also like blanks, they can be harmful and painful. Therefore, if an actor wears a squib, make sure he has the proper padding between the squib blasts and his skin.

Fire and explosions add realism to any film but they are expensive to mount. Filming them will require the services of a certified explosives expert and a fire marshal (often a retired firefighter). Large fires or blasts will mandate a fire truck and several emergency technicians. Furthermore, these scenarios go hand-in-hand with a mound of costly insurance. In other words, this is no situation for guerilla filmmaking. Exploding buildings and cars are probably out of your price range. No matter how remote your location, do not attempt large blazes or blasts without a safety expert on set. Don't play with fire, kids.

Weather effects on a large scale are difficult for even a studio film to create, but small weather effects can be achieved easily. For example, during an interior shot, you can make it appear to be raining outside a window by using a simple water sprinkler and adding some post-production sounds. Similarly, snow outside a window can be faked by sifting artificial snow through a grate. (For those of you on an ultra-low-budget, you can use corn flakes painted white or bits of paper.) Lightning strikes can be done with flashing lights. Wind can be added to any shot by utilizing electric fans. If it's kept to a cozy minimum, don't fear fake weather.

On the other hand, significant climate effects, as well as real rain, lightning, snow and strong winds (all of which can easily destroy an exterior shoot) should chill you to the bone.

Special makeup effects can generally be achieved cheaply—if not always effectively. Stage blood can be bought at a costume store or you can whip it up in your own kitchen.

**GRANDMA'S
OLD-FASHIONED HOMEMADE BLOOD**
Tasty alone or great on pancakes.
Ingredients: Clear Syrup; Water; Red and Black Food Coloring (more red than black; coffee grounds can be substituted for black food coloring)
Directions: Mix to the desired consistency and shade of crimson.

Other effects, such as scary monster scars or wrinkled skin for aging effects, may require the expertise of a makeup professional. Avoid that cheesy Halloween look. Don't forget: the big screen magnifies every fake tooth and clump of hair. If your special makeup is less than special, limit its screen time.

Special photographic effects, such as **animation, miniatures, matte shots** (background paintings that look like locations) and **blue screen** (subjects shot in front of a blank blue or green screen so that they can later be inserted into another location, such as an actor superimposed against a sky to make it appear he's flying) are best done by effects houses. You can try any of these on a shoestring budget; believability is another matter. Miniatures, for example, don't necessarily require a large investment, but if done cheaply or by an inexperienced hand, they run the risk of looking like those found in laughable sci-fi B-movies of old. Consult early with effects or optical houses to see if you can fit special photographic FX into your budget.

Stock footage of previously-made effects can be your answer to expensive miniatures and effects, but make sure such film can be seamlessly incorporated into the footage you shoot.

Computer generated images (CGI) have exploded onto the film scene in recent years and are responsible for pushing some studio film budgets over the $100,000,000 range. Many computer effects are not possible without a budget in the millions. But the digital FX world is a rapidly changing place. The sort of images that now can be created on a *relatively* small system, at a *relatively* inexpensive cost, are amazing. With the right connections, you may be able to fit some computer FX into your low-budget film. The slower processing CGI machines are the cheapest to use, but they could take months to get the images right. Late summer is generally the downtime for digital houses; their rates are often more flexible at this time. You might also consider using a freelancer with his own system. Some of these artists are creating cutting-edge effects just for the fun of it, and they may be happy to work for little or no money if it means their art will be seen.

Stunts may or may not require the services of an official stunt person. Fights, tumbles and shoot-'em-ups can be staged with energetic actors, a few pillows and a mattress. Others cannot (or should not) be attempted by anyone who is not a professional fall guy or gal.

Car crashes are a relatively common movie occurrence, but they have a high quotient of danger. If your movie calls for anything more than a fender bender, you'll need an experienced stunt driver behind the wheel and emergency personnel standing by.

Falls and jumps from more than a one-story height are hazardous and, needless to say, will require a fall person, stunt coordinator and all the necessary safety devices.

Any dangerous act will drastically increase your insurance budget (and you should never stage death-defying feats without the proper coverage). Use your judgment when it comes to crashes and falls. If injury is a possibility, hire a stuntperson and bear the expense; write the stunt out of your script; or alter it so that a fall becomes a tumble or a crash becomes a thump. Sound effects can always be added later.

With all special effects and stunts, you should know before production begins whether or not you have the budget to convincingly pull them off. If you can't, don't try to slide by with something less than authentic. Nothing will kill audience believability faster than laughable FX or lame stunts. When it comes to visual trickery, today's audiences are spoiled by Hollywood mega-budgets. Studio films have raised the FX bar and, low-budget or not, you want to compete for some of the same ticket buyers as the studios. Don't let the spectators see the strings above the spaceship or the punches being pulled; don't let them spot the rabbit up your sleeve. And if you can't hide the rabbit, don't try the magic.

DAILIES

During filming, the director tells the script supervisor which takes he would like to see printed; the script supervisor circles these take numbers. The second camera assistant and the sound mixer also make notes for the lab. The lab develops the negatives of only the **circled takes**, thus saving you the cost of printing every take you shoot. If you're editing on a nonlinear system, the lab will then transfer these takes onto videotape. You should be able to view these dailies (also called "rushes") the next day. Hopefully, you and the cinematographer will also have the opportunity to watch some developed film footage projected on a big screen.

Rushes give the director and producer the ability to see how performances are translating to the screen, to evaluate the visual look and to get a partial feel for how the film is coming together. Dailies are also of great value to the cinematographer, who, in addition to assessing camera work, lighting, etc., can appraise the lab's processing work. Other crew members, especially the first camera assistant, gaffer, dolly grip, makeup artist and sound mixer can benefit from seeing and hearing this footage. Let them watch. Dailies usually are a crew morale booster.

Whether or not the actors should view dailies is a long-standing question. Most experts maintain that actors become self-conscious when they see themselves on film, therefore, the logic follows that actors should not watch dailies. Instead, all performers should trust the director fully. On the other hand, with video dailies readily available on or near the set (as opposed to the old days when filmmakers had to go to screening rooms to watch film dailies), it's harder to keep the cast from seeing them. Too, preventing them from watching dailies may feed their insecurities and doubts. So the debate continues. Whatever you decide, keep your decision standard and equal for all performers.

16/DIRECTING A MOVIE

It's impossible to tell someone how to be a great director, just as it is impossible to teach someone how to be a great painter, writer or composer. Creative greatness comes from someplace other than books and lectures. True greatness comes from transcending that which has been accomplished before. Having said that, you must master the basics of filmmaking before you can hope to be good— or great. Learn all you can:

- Read about all aspects of filmmaking, including theory and history.

- Educate yourself to cinema's related fields, such as theater, photography and literature.

- Take as many worthwhile classes as you can.

- Watch as many movies as you can. Study the editing, shot selection, acting, staging, lighting. Listen carefully to the music. Note how certain camera moves or color schemes or sounds affect you emotionally, almost subconsciously.

- Take acting classes or sit in on acting workshops.

- Practice directing in any way you can: storyboard or diagram shots, work with performers, plot invisible movies in your mind.

- Dream. To direct a film is to capture a dream.

COMMUNICATION

Communication is paramount to directing. You must be able to convey exactly what you want to the cast and crew and in a manner that allows everyone to work to his fullest potential. The director is the coach, the conductor, the general. Make sure your word is final. This doesn't mean you can't accept advice; it simply means that you must remain in control of all creative decisions. You'll need to be able to answer a hundred questions a day—swiftly and with confidence.

There is a clear and distinct **chain of command** on a film set. The director (*general*) is the one person who guides the actors (*the elite guard*). The director will also issue instructions to the cinematographer (*colonel*) and assistant director (*lieutenant colonel*). The cinematographer commands the gaffer and key grip (*captains*) who in turn are in charge of the electricians and grips (*soldiers*). The assistant director makes sure everyone in the crew/platoon does his job. The director will speak often with the sound mixer and the script supervisor (*captains*). The mixer oversees the boom operator (*private*). All officers can command the production assistants (*recruits*).

On most sets, the chain of command is unstated. Keep it loose so that anyone can speak to anyone else. Foster a family atmosphere. In this vein, always refer to your film as "our" movie, not "my" movie. But when it comes to signing off on decisions, make sure a clear hierarchy is maintained: only one person—you, the director—gives the marching orders and dictates the ultimate battle strategy.

On the set, before each scene is shot, a series of procedures takes place:

1) the a.d. quiets everybody down ("Quiet on the set!");

2) the sound recorder announces he's ready ("Speed!");

3) the camera is turned on ("We're rolling!");

4) the camera assistant slates the take;

5) the director shouts, "Action!"

When the take is done or if it needs to be stopped before completion, the director calls, "Cut!" You may also have an agreement with the camera operator, cinematographer and sound mixer: if any one of them detects an irreversible problem (such as an out-of-focus camera, a boom in the frame or constant, unwanted noise) they can yell "Cut!" This shouldn't happen often, but when it does, it can save valuable time and film stock. Alternately, you can have an agreement with your crew members that any one of them should point out problems to you immediately so that you— and only you—have the option of halting a take.

Besides having a good working relationship with the d.p. and a.d., of equal importance to the director is the shepherding, guiding and cajoling of actors toward the best possible performance. The director-actor relationship is based on confidence and trust. An actor can feel very vulnerable knowing (or hoping, in the case of an independent film) that his face will be projected forty feet wide and viewed by millions of strangers. Therefore, you must make him confident in you as a director and in himself as an actor.

During the rehearsal stage, if not during casting, you need to discover how each actor approaches his craft. The **Method** actor wants to "become" a role, to actually experience his character's emotions and thoughts. It's not always easy or desirable for the actor to turn his performance on and off. The **Technical** actor relies on certain tactics, such as studying his character's motivations. There are sub-groups of technical actors who work with various philosophies and techniques. What playwright-director David Mamet praises as the **"direct"** actor who performs the action or says the line without distracting himself with motives or a broader context.

Sometimes there are conflicts between actors who utilize different techniques. It's your job to mediate and smooth these differences. Have respect for each performer's working style and make sure that the crew and other cast members share this respect. When actors are on set and in character, you and the a.d. should keep the crew reasonably quiet to allow the actors to concentrate.

Learn how to influence performance. Usually, this will mean staying positive and gently guiding actors towards the appropriate result, as opposed to offering harsh criticism or telling them what to feel or what to do. But there are no set rules. Some actors need more guidance than others. Some need to be built up and pampered. Some would prefer being left alone. Others need to be motivated or provoked. The closest thing to a general rule is this: Most actors are insecure; direct them.

As the coach, conductor, general—as the *director*—you need to be able to communicate freely with everyone, from executive producer to p.a. It may not be easy, but manage every question and every crisis with a smile. Never lose you cool. And always know what you're doing . . . or pretend like you do.

COVERAGE

When you step on the set, you should have a definite strategy for covering the script so that you can capture, during the hectic weeks of production, all the shots you need to have in order to tell your story correctly. Here's where all your planning pays off. Here's where you'll utilize your shooting script, shot lists, diagrams and storyboards (see "SCHEDULE: Shooting Strategy").

The most efficient order of shots in a scene is usually from largest to smallest. There are three reasons for this:

1. The longest take—the master shot—establishes a scene's overall look and lighting pattern. By starting with a master shot and moving in for closer coverage, you and the cinematographer will have to worry less about lighting continuity than if you go from close-ups to progressively wider shots.

2. Getting the master shot first gives you the peace of mind of knowing that everything in a scene has been covered. If you're running behind schedule, you may need to drop tighter shots or rush through them, but with a master, you'll know that, at the very least, you have all the lines and action on film.

3. A master shot establishes continuity in dialogue, small actions and blocking. By doing the longest shot first, the cast will have a context for their words and actions when they repeat them in tighter shots. Also, the crew will know what is taking place later and they can watch for continuity problems as the coverage gets progressively closer.

Rarely is a master shot perfect, but don't repeat entire masters unless more than half of the take has been ruined. Master shots require a lot of valuable film, most of which you'll probably never use. Instruct the actors not to stop if they flub a line. In fact, they should never stop until they hear you say, "Cut!" Most things will be covered again; if they aren't, you can pick up the necessary flubbed line or action from the master setup before moving on.

Having explained the benefits of master shots, here comes the plot twist: you can, occasionally, forget about them. If you're absolutely certain that you'll never use a master of a particular scene, skip it. Even considering the positives listed here, the significant expenses of time and film stock may outweigh the benefit of shooting such a long shot. If you choose to shoot a dialogue scene without a master, make certain there are multiple takes of line readings in case one is unusable. Also, you still should do wider shots before close-ups, to better establish continuity.

Shooting without a master involves "editing-in-camera." As mentioned earlier, this means you have an exact idea of what the film will look like when edited so that you know precisely what to shoot. This way, you won't waste time and money filming stuff you'll never use. Many indies are shot in this manner.

When covering scenes, don't skimp! Studio flicks usually shoot everything from a variety of different angles, with a number of different lenses, etc.; all this coverage is then sorted out in the editing room. They do this because they can afford to. Low-budget filmmakers, however, with one eye on their limited shooting ratio and the other on their 100-page script, often try to get by with one long shot covering three pages or more. The problem with a mega-take like this is that a shot might seem great during production, but later, when you're in the editing room trying to fit it into the broader context of your film, it can seem too long or (less likely) too short or you may suddenly discover a head-slapping error right smack in the middle of it! If you haven't covered yourself by taking close-ups, reaction shots, two-shots, etc., you will be stuck with things the way they are.

A variety of coverage gives you alternatives. You can shorten a take of a scene. You can lengthen it. You can use part of one long take, cut away, and then use part of a different long take. Such options are crucial during the editing process. A variety of coverage can't make a bad movie great, but it can make a bad movie adequate and a good movie better.

Unless you're Alfred Hitchcock, no matter how much planning you do and no matter how much in-camera editing you do, your movie probably will not take shape until post-production. Don't eliminate your choices during editing by severely constricting your coverage during production.

Another technique that will make your film better-edited is **overlapping action**. Cutting on movement creates a more seamless edit. Therefore, during production, maximize your footage at the beginning and end of action shots. For example, if (in two separate shots) a woman walks to a rock, sits down and sings, have her walk and sit down in the first shot, then sit and sing in the second. In this way, you can cut on the action of the actor sitting and distract us from the edit, making it virtually invisible.

Similar to overlapping action is the technique of letting the subject completely exit one frame and enter an empty frame. This is called, appropriately, **"clearing the frame,"** and it can be used in place of cutting on action. It also allows you to show the same subject in front of a different background in subsequent shots, to illustrate the passage of time.

Shots are the *"words"* with which directors communicate on film; they convey specific meanings. Strung together, these *words* form *"sentences"* and *"paragraphs"* and, eventually, a complete story. Make sure that, during production, you find the correct *words* to express the desired emotions. For example, if you want to show the pain on someone's face, you'll most probably need a close-up; make sure you get the close-up. You don't want to be in the editing room and find that you have only wide shots to express this kind of emotional moment.

SHOT LEXICON

As sort of a lexicon of filmmaking *"words,"* the following is a glossary of the basic shots:

- **Establishing shot** shows a general environment; it often presents a character in relation to his surroundings.

- **Master shot** covers the whole scene (or a significant portion of it), usually from a wide angle.

- **Wide shot** (WS) (or *full shot*) shows a full character, usually from head to toe, or a significant portion of a location.

- **Two-shot** (2S) shows two characters. **Three-shot** (3S) shows three. **Four-shot** (4S) shows four. **Group shot** shows more than four characters.

- **Over-the-shoulder** (OTS) is about the same size as a medium shot, but part of one character (usually some of his shoulder and the side of his head) is in the foreground as he faces the principal subject.

- **Medium shot** (MS) typically shows a character from the waist up. Medium shots are a good size for most dialogue scenes.

- **Close-up** (CU) usually shows a character's face only. Close-ups are best for presenting expressions, thoughts and emotions.

- **Extreme close-up** (ECU) typically is so close that only part of a person's face fits in the frame. ECUs are ideal for showing emotions.

- **Pan** moves the camera on an axis, to the left or to the right.

- **Tilt** moves the camera on an axis, up or down.

- **Tracking shot** (or **dolly shot**) moves the entire camera forward, backward, left or right.

- **Crane shot** moves the entire camera (on a dolly or crane) up or down.

- **Zoom** adjusts the focal length of the lens to optically bring us closer (zoom in) or take us away (zoom out).

- **Low angle** is a shot that looks up. This generally makes a person seem more powerful.

- **High angle** is a shot that looks down. This generally makes someone appear more vulnerable.

- **Dutch angle** is a shot made when the camera is slanted at an angle. This usually makes the things feel out of kilter.

- **P.O.V.** (point of view) is a shot from a specific character's perspective, making us see what he sees.

- **Hand-held** is footage shot while holding the camera. This often has an unsteady or documentary feel.

- **Steadicam** is a moving shot made with a camera harnessed to an operator (with a steadying device). A Steadicam allows for more mobile tracking shots.

- **Insert** is a stand-alone shot (often a close-up of an object) that is placed within the main action.

A variety of these shots can be used in combination with each other. Know your filmmaking language. Be able to speak fluently in the preceding terms in order to convey your plans to the cinematographer, editor and others in the crew.

STYLE

Easy to define but difficult to attain, style is the personality of your film. Style is conveyed through all the means at your disposal: words, actions, performers, locales, lighting, makeup, decor, color, camera movement, lenses, editing, sound effects, music, opticals—everything. The director has a tremendous amount of tools with which to work. Mastering all of them could take a lifetime. But mastering them isn't even the most important thing.

You can read books, take classes and go to seminars on directing. You can study every conceivable camera movement and memorize each technical term. You can acquire invaluable information at acting classes and become increasingly more confident working with performers. You can learn about editing and music and production design. And you should do all of these things and many more. But you cannot truly be trained in the two things you—as a director—need more than any other: a **great story** (covered in the "SCRIPT" section) and a **strong vision** (your interpretation of the story). Filmmaking is a creative art and no one can tell you how to be creative. Blaze your own path—but know where you're going. You may have dreamed of making a movie for so long that you're bursting with ideas. Now it is crucial for you to focus your energies into one coherent vision. Do not let a quest for originality overtake your best-laid plans. The indie world is full of overreaching, pretentious, first films. Make sure your style serves your story. If you've written a Southern melodrama, *El Mariachi*-paced rapid-fire coverage and editing will most probably not suit your story well; neither will an action picture be best served with the laid-back feeling of *Stranger Than Paradise*.

You—the director with the vision—are the one person who should always have the big picture in mind. Everyone else plays a smaller role to aid you in capturing this vision. While they concentrate on performing their particular jobs to the best of their abilities, you must make sure that the end result adds up to your vision.

What should that vision be? One of the hardest aspects of filmmaking is to establish your own distinctive style. There aren't many directors who have one. But those who do, have it because those qualities that make them unique also serve their stories. It is a rare occasion when you can effectively, consciously force a style on a film. Style, if it happens at all, needs to come naturally.

Meanwhile, marshal all the cinematic tools at your disposal. Fully utilize every technique to interpret your story and to convey your vision.

17/SAVING A MOVIE

Perhaps the most important factors for successfully shepherding a film through production are preventing and managing crises. Things can go wrong during a shoot that can destroy everything you've worked for and devour every dollar you've raised. Be aware of potential problems now and do everything you can to prevent them from materializing later. But if a problem does occur, be ready, willing and able to solve it as quickly and thoroughly as possible. Your film depends on it.

PICKUPS

Pickups (also called **retakes**) are shots that are filmed out of the normal shooting schedule, usually at the end of the shoot or after production wraps. Pickups are made because the quality of the original shot is questionable or because during the editing process, you discover that you need a particular shot in order to assemble the best possible sequence.

With nonlinear editing, the editor is now able to assemble a rough cut during production; therefore, the ability exists to identify possible pickup shots early. If the editor has a problem with every take of a specific line, if he is unable to properly assemble the footage with the existing shots; or if he just feels a certain shot would make a sequence cut smoother, he can convey this message to you during the shoot. Then, instead of reassembling the cast and crew (if possible) and re-renting the equipment and location(s) (if possible)— all at great expense—you can get the pickups before wrapping.

Juggling pickups into the end of an already short and tight schedule isn't easy. For this reason, plan ahead. Remember the recommendation to make the first day of production lighter than the rest? Similarly, the last day or two of production should be slimmer than those in the middle, thus giving you time to shoot a few pickups or catch up on your schedule if you're running behind.

Don't compromise other footage to do retakes unless it is absolutely necessary; redressing and lighting sets to match footage shot a week before can take hours. Close-ups are the easiest pickups to get because, with the foreground filled, a little ingenuity can make almost any background look like an earlier location.

If, in the editing room months after wrapping, you discover that you need a few more shots, don't despair. You can often get a limited cast and the principal crew members to work for a day for free. After all, they have an interest in your film succeeding. Cameras and locations can also frequently be managed for little or no money if you need them for only a day (or less). Keep any unrented props or costumes (after wrapping) in case they're required for retakes.

If you need more than two days of pickups after wrapping, it can be quite expensive. But if you must have the shots, find a way to get them—even if it means going into debt. Remember: A bad film (even if it comes in on budget and on schedule) is virtually worthless while a good film (that may have gone over budget and over schedule) may launch your career.

SCHEDULING PROBLEMS
To extend the shooting schedule for even a day will cost you considerably in salaries, catering and equipment rental fees. And, even if you can afford it, your cast and crew may have lined up other jobs; cameras and lights may have been reserved to go elsewhere; the necessary ingredients may be unavailable for an extra day.

If your production cannot keep up with the schedule, you must address the root cause of the problem as soon as it surfaces and try to remedy it. Is it an actor? (An attitude can sometimes be adjusted.) A crew member? (An unmotivated crew member can be replaced.) Is it because of equipment failure? (Equipment can be fixed or exchanged.) Weather conditions? (Plan for alternative, interior locations.) Is it a combination of these problems?

All of the above problems are common, but the most likely low-budget schedule-busters are an overly ambitious number of setups per day and/or the simple grind of production taking its toll on a limited crew. These things can only be remedied by changing your ways and reducing your workload.

When falling behind, you must find methods to make up lost hours. And this can be a quandary. If you haven't maintained the original schedule, it is foolhardy to believe you can maintain it for the remainder of the shoot—*and* create painless ways to make up significant time. It's never painless. Get real. And get cutting.

Trimming dialogue can eliminate some setups and save you a few hours, but to make up a half a day or more, you'll need to scrap entire scenes and locations. This does not necessarily mean ripping material from your script. Often, scenes in different areas of one location (as in the kitchen or the bedroom of a house) which would require new setups can be shot in the same room, thus rescuing hours. Remember: moving and setting up at different sites takes more time than anything else your crew does. Many scenes can be shot in any generic location. Contemplate getting them at or near the location of another scene.

A few more time-saving tips:

- Night footage is usually harder to light than day footage. An evening scene might be changed to an afternoon scene or shot "day for night" (in daylight but made to look like moonlight) to save significant lighting time.

- Movement takes time. Contrary to the tenets of filmmaking which preach motion in the frame, you may need to cut dolly shots and/or keep actors more stationary. For example, dialogue in a traveling car (often a difficult setup) can be changed to a stationary location, such as a parked car.

- A dramatic event, such as a violent crime, can take place off-screen (sometimes to greater effect) and be signified by a sound (scream, gunshot, music . . .). Great low-budget movies throughout history (including many classic film noirs) have utilized this technique.

- Cramped spaces are harder to light and to work in. You may need to "open up" a scene. For example, if you have a shoot-out taking place on a staircase, move it to a rooftop.

- Exteriors are usually easier to light than interiors, but watch for sunlight continuity.

- Generally, the more people in a scene, the more time it takes to light them and to direct them. Can you eliminate some actors/extras from shots? Can you turn a big party into an intimate get-together?

- Wider shots usually take more time to light than medium shots or close-ups. You may need to substitute tighter shots for wide ones.

- A carefully-monitored production report can help you discern where things slow down. Note what types of setups and shots take the longest, what time of day and days of the week your crew works the fastest, etc., and adjust your schedule accordingly.

- A small second camera unit (perhaps using a camera unsynced for sound) can be used to get footage at the same time that you're shooting the main action with first unit. This is an especially effective way of shooting pickups, inserts and establishing shots.

An actor may have to lose his favorite line; your cinematographer may not get that dolly shot he wanted; your production designer may dress a set that you'll never use. But stick to your guns. If things have to go, they have to go.

If you must make adjustments, make them early, when you have the maximum number of options. If you wait until the final week of production to address the fact that you're two days behind schedule, you'll either have a movie with less-than-ideal footage or you'll risk going over-budget to extend the schedule.

BUDGET PROBLEMS

Almost by their definition, nonstudio movies have financial problems. As mentioned previously, sometimes they are caused by going over schedule. Another common mistake is shooting more film than planned. Remember: in addition to the hefty price of film stock, there is the large expense of having it developed. (If you're going to go over budget anywhere, this is the place to do it, as the money spent for more takes and increased coverage is seen on the screen. But, extra film stock is a luxury most under-financed indies cannot afford.)

If you need to reduce the amount of film being utilized, you must consciously limit your number of takes and/or reduce your coverage. You can conserve a little by calling, "Action!" the second the camera and sound recorder are ready and by yelling, "Cut!" the second you know that a take is completed. In addition, limit the number of takes to be developed and transferred to video. Circle only the best one or two. Later, in the editing room, if you'd like to look at other choices, you can always have more takes transferred to video (for a stiff fee, of course).

In addition to lengthened schedules and film stock overruns, budget crunches come from any number of reasons: equipment breaking; locations becoming unavailable; rain falling on your parade. When you're dealing with a few tons of complex gear, a cast and crew of twenty or more and a variety of locations and outside forces, things go wrong. Anticipate problems.

Predicaments often force you to scramble. And when you scramble, you invariably must pay more—sometimes much more—for equipment, services and locations. Therefore, the more difficulties you anticipate, the less scrambling and spending you'll have to do.

If you can afford it, you should write into your budget a contingency equivalent to five to ten percent of your total budget. Bonding companies will require the higher figure before issuing a completion bond (necessary for most bank loans); and experienced producers and unit production managers always want as big a contingency as possible to protect their reputations against going over-budget. They know things will probably go wrong, and they anticipate having to pay for the unexpected. Insurance is another good precaution against the expenses of catastrophes, big and small (see "PAPERWORK: Insurance").

Wherever you are during production, make sure the producer and u.p.m. have the **phone numbers, fax numbers** and **addresses** for all rental houses, labs, insurance agencies, caterers, stock distributors and any other establishments you're doing business with, as well as alternate resources that you're not currently using. In addition, the producer, u.p.m. and probably the assistant director should have—at all times—**emergency contact numbers** (police, fire, paramedic) and directions to the nearest hospital. And, what's a telephone number without a telephone? The production should buy, rent or borrow at least one cellular phone for the duration of the shoot (or, make sure there's a phone available at every location).

So, you've planned for the worse. What do you do when it happens? First of all, don't panic. Don't let the situation explode your budget. Never appear desperate (even though you probably will be), especially when talking to vendors. No matter how dire your situation, always try to shop for a bargain.

Of course, you're going to try not to let any crisis send you over-budget but, if you must, you can regroup and refinance between production and post-production. As was mentioned with pickups, it is much more desirable to get a good film in the can and go into debt than it is to compromise your vision and end up with a bad or mediocre film that was completed within its budget. Worry about post-production financing later; for now, concentrate on the shoot only. Focus on making (in order) the best film for the least amount of money.

PEOPLE PROBLEMS

The producer, director, cinematographer and assistant director must be maestros at managing divergent personalities. Film productions are often a volatile mix of artists, technicians and egos. On studio productions, the mix may be even greater but everything is cushioned by a blanket of money. On low-budget shoots, where everyone is underpaid and overworked, there is no such cushion. And, sometimes, the volatile components don't mix at all.

If problems erupt, isolate them. Deal with them one-on-one and in a calm setting. Know when to compromise and when to stand firm. If cast and crew members, as a group, have an unreasonable grievance, your best strategy is to divide and conquer. Emphasize "the family unity" needed to make an independent film; reiterate that everyone will benefit from a well-made film; break individuals away from the pack; isolate any holdout.

If you have to fire someone for the good of the movie, do it. It's not ideal, of course, but any crew member can be replaced. Needless to say, cutting your lead actor is not as easy as firing a grip. Work things out. As the director, take no sides, but make each person feel that you're on his side. A principal cast or crew member may flaunt the leverage he has, thinking you can't afford to lose him. If you have to, gently let him know that he can't afford to lose you; casting directors and producers would hear about it. Directors rarely have time to be babysitters. Someone else (probably a producer) will need to smooth things out when the director's time is scarce.

Sickness costs time and money. Recommend that your cast and crew take vitamins (especially C), eat well and get plenty of sleep (stagger call times). Actors can nap or rest when not on the set. If a lead becomes seriously ill, figure a way to shoot around him for a day or two. After that, they need to get in front of the camera. Actors must see their job through to the end.

WRAP

When your movie has been shot, wrapping it will consist of returning all rented or borrowed items to the appropriate people and businesses. This may take a day or more. Hopefully, you've kept careful track of who owns what. **Breaking and missing** charges (the total cost of broken or lost items) may have to be paid. If you're under-insured or uninsured, pray that every item checks in perfectly, especially the camera.

Leftover negative stock and many expendables have value. Film stock can be sold to resale distributors or directly to interested buyers (see "STOCK: Shopping: Gray Market"). It will fetch the highest price if it was never taken out of the can. Your sound mixer might offer to pay for any leftover audio stock. Otherwise, it also can be sold on the gray market. Certain expendables, especially gels, can be sold to equipment houses or directly to gaffers and cinematographers.

Someone should store all necessary props and costumes that weren't rented. Keep them at least until picture editing is complete (and ideally, through distribution), in case you need an item to appear on camera in a pickup shot. Also, if your film is released, certain items may have marketing or collecting value.

When everyone has recovered from the strain of production, throw a big blast, a shindig, a gala, a fiesta—a **wrap party**. Your cast and crew will deserve it and such an event will help them forgive you for those final, seventeen-hour days.

POST-PRODUCTION

18/PICTURE EDITING

It's a funny thing about film: you take a series of scenes, maybe five scenes, and perhaps there are twenty-five different ways you can put those five scenes together five at a time, and there's probably only one way that makes any sense, and you've got to find that one way. The others are meaningless.

— Frank Capra

It's appropriate that "editing," a word most associated with written compositions, is used to describe the process of assembling a movie because the essence of film editing is writing with pictures.

Editing is taking the *"words"* (shots) that you created in production and stringing them into *"sentences"* (sequences) and *"paragraphs"* (scenes) to tell your story. Your original ideas about "picture writing" may change along the way; never be afraid to rewrite.

TECHNIQUE
When editing, you and your editor should always consider the movie as a whole. Inventive and flashy sequences are great but they should be used only if they serve the overall vision of the story.

There are certain techniques, developed over the years, that viewers have come to accept (mostly subconsciously) as part of the language of filmmaking. You would do well to make them part of your *"grammar"* now. Here are a few general *"writing"*/editing rules:

- Try to cut on motion. It is much easier to disguise edits when they occur during movement.

151

- Each cut should have a dramatic purpose, however slight.

- In most cases, editing should be "invisible." Cuts should feel natural and not draw attention to themselves.

- Do not cut directly from one shot of a subject to another similar shot of the same subject: the image will jump and look like a mistake. If you must use two shots of the same subject that are not significantly different in size or angle, edit a different shot between them.

- Watch for eye lines, center lines and any other potential continuity problems.

- When there is not enough footage to overcome continuity gaps, use a **cutaway** (a shot not directly involving the main action) to bridge the edit. That said, avoid obvious cutaways, which often look sloppy.

These rules are not hard and fast: legendary independent director Jean-Luc Godard has proven this with his style of **jump cut** editing (purposely rough edits) and with his general disregard for common standards of continuity. However, unless you're very sure of what you're doing and why you're doing it, do not try to make your film more edgy with *avant-garde* cutting. It's best to obey the language laws of editing. Audiences depend on them.

Pace (or *rhythm*) is crucial in assembling a movie. Making a scene or sequence play longer or shorter can generate specific effects. Pacing is accomplished through the length of scenes (and, indeed, of the entire film) and through the number of cuts (the more cuts, the faster scenes tend to play). The acceleration of the tempo of edits (as opposed to a continuous quick rate of cutting) will create a sense of urgency. Be aware of the pace at all times and make sure it's appropriate throughout.

The first assemblage of film is called the **rough cut**. The editor might compile this rough assembly of scenes without the director's guidance; in these days of computerized editing, a rough cut can often be created while the film is in production.

Seeing your film in sequence for the first time may be sobering. Don't worry yet. It's called a rough cut for a reason. Subsequently, you and the editor will assemble several more versions. Each time, the film will get closer to its final glory (it also will usually get shorter). Your editor should be able to show you several options for editing each scene and you might suggest a few more. As the director, you always have the final say. Respect the editor's expertise, but remember: he works for you. While he may suggest and consult, he is hired to carry out your wishes.

Never depend on the promise of music or sound effects to rescue a scene. A sequence should be better with these accompaniments, but don't count on it. Make it work now and it should only get better when the soundtrack is complete.

As the film approaches its final cut, get some outside opinions, especially from people who have no familiarity with the story. They will see the full film from a fresh perspective. However hard you strive to keep your focus on the overall vision, you'll invariably get caught up in the details of your movie. You may be surprised to learn that most viewers won't even notice the little things that you're obsessing over (which isn't to say the little things aren't important— they often work on a subliminal level). They will see the film as a whole and that should be your main concern.

NONLINEAR

Nonlinear editing has been referred to throughout this book because it is now the industry standard. "Nonlinear" essentially means "computerized."

The film you shoot will be transferred to videotape (usually in 3/4" or Beta SP format; see "LAB, PART 1"). The information contained on the video is then **digitized** into the memory of a computer. Once there, every take can easily and quickly be lifted, moved, sliced and placed next to another to create a movie—all without being touched by human hands. When you're absolutely satisfied with the assembled film, the list of edits is outputted from the computer; this is used by the lab to cut the negative.

The two most popular nonlinear editing systems today are *AVID* (*Mac*-based, used with a mouse) and *Lightworks* (favored by old-school editors because of its *Moviola*-like controller). *D-Vision* and others are cheaper but less powerful. Before hiring your editor, make sure he is very familiar with the particular system you plan to use.

Hopefully, someone will have connections that will help you rent a nonlinear system at a fraction of the standard rates. Play up the fact that you're an independent filmmaker. Many production companies have systems that go unused at night or in the early morning hours, so you may be able to edit your film during these graveyard shifts. If you're bereft of a connection, if you're unable to find an unused or little-used system or if you cannot wrangle a good discount, expect to pay between $1,000 to $2,000 per week.

Various optical effects (fades, slow-motion, wipes, etc.) can be performed on nonlinear systems. These may look great on the computer monitor but when you go to film, you will still need to have them done by an optical house at significant expense. Make sure you can afford optical effects later or don't put them in now.

Audio work can also be accomplished on a nonlinear system, including cleaning and equalizing of dialogue and inserting of sound effects and music. If you're tight on cash, you can do a decent sound edit on a nonlinear system. However, because the audio tracks will be edited on their own, don't waste time trying to perfect the audio now; at this point, simply clean it up by eliminating distractions to attain a sense of how the visuals play with the sound.

A video can be output at any time from a nonlinear system. This allows you to "print" a rough assembly, first cut, etc., take it home, watch it alone, play it in slow-motion, screen it for friends, and carefully analyze every aspect in an environment other than the editing room. Take full advantage of this.

When it comes time to create your final copy, most machines cannot make a broadcast-quality video, so one option is to transfer your data to a more expensive nonlinear system—one with "on-line capabilities"—and output from there. Better yet, schedule an actual **on-line session.** A technician will take your original tapes and, armed with a computerized list of cuts, he will construct a master, video to video, with virtually no loss of resolution. In fact, with color correction, the quality of the master is frequently better than that of the original video. This is how tapes are made for television broadcast. But, this process is usually very expensive. Shop for a bargain, but an actual on-line session may be out of your price range.

Make sure your master video is made in either Beta SP or 3/4" videotape format. Have a second copy made (the quality of this is less important) with visible time coding, to be used when doing the sound editing.

LINEAR

Linear editing is about as low-budget as you can get. It's virtually free. But linear editing is not without its own steep costs: a huge investment of time and a possible expenditure of all your patience.

After your takes are transferred to video, you can actually edit them into a motion picture utilizing only two VCRs. You play the transfer video in one VCR and record the shots you want in sequence onto a tape in the other VCR. This sounds easy enough until you realize that whenever something is not right or whenever you want to alter a scene, you must go to that point in your movie-in-progress, change it and then change *everything after it* all over again! *Every time!* When you finally finish editing, you then must manually make note of the precise times and coding numbers for every shot (these must be accurate!) in order for a lab to properly cut your negative.

You may not believe anyone would have the patience to cut a feature film this way, but it has been done successfully. Robert Rodriguez edited *El Mariachi* (a movie with frenetic cutting) with just a couple of VCRs. The low-budget indies *What Happened Was . . .* and *Swoon* were also assembled in this low-tech fashion.

If you know exactly what you're doing, if you don't have much footage to sift through (Rodriguez had only four hours), if you keep careful notes and, most importantly, if you do as many changes as possible before recutting (so that you only have to completely re-edit the movie a few times, as opposed to having to go from each cut to the end many times), well, it can be done. It seems like an unbearably difficult process, but it is a possibility.

If you're flat broke and have no other options, it won't cost you anything to try to edit your film this way (assuming you have access to two VCRs). Otherwise, pay the money and save your sanity: cut on a nonlinear system.

"OLD SCHOOL"

Ahh, the good old days of Steenbecks and Mylar splice tape; trim bins and foot pedals; strips of film attached to cords with clothes pins. Long hours in cramped quarters. You still can cut your film in the traditional fashion, of course. But the techniques are growing closer and closer to extinction. In this computer age, the editing bed is going the way of the manual typewriter: a novelty, still used, but almost exclusively by those who simply refuse to adapt to new technology.

The equipment can be rented or bought cheaply (now more than ever). You'll save money by not having your film transferred to video but you'll spend money having it processed. The reason editing on a flatbed is considered cost-prohibitive is because of the time it requires. Unless you plan to cut the film yourself (that is, if you have six months to spare), you'll need to hire an editor to work ten weeks or more (twice as long and twice as expensive as for nonlinear editing) and at least one full-time assistant editor (which nonlinear does not require). Before you can even make one edit, it takes two weeks for two editors to manually synchronize all the sound rolls with the developed film. (You can have a first cut on a nonlinear system by then.)

In addition, editing Super 16 on film can create problems when it comes to projecting the completed cut. Make sure your lab has a Super 16 projector available so you can view work prints. You won't want to cut the negative having only seen your dream film on a Moviola. The inability to insert opticals or music or sound effects while editing the picture (these things are done later) is another distinct disadvantage to the "old-school" method.

Still, if you're itching to handle the film yourself, to get right into the thick of it and watch it roll by—frame by frame—locate a Moviola or similar flatbed system and go for it. But most of us should move beyond foot pedals and splice tape; take advantage of modern technology.

19/MUSIC

Music is one of the most important, yet least appreciated, components of filmmaking. It conveys information, expresses emotions, establishes moods and aids in maintaining continuity by bridging scenes and shots. Additionally, on low-budget productions, it helps disguise imperfections in the dialogue and effects tracks.

For all these reasons, no matter how small your budget, try to have the musical score completed correctly before showing your film to buyers or submitting it to festivals. It's best not to delay the music in the hopes of getting more money later. If you don't have the money to score it now, where will you get the cash to score it later? If the distributor puts up the money, they may have their own ideas about music; try to do it your way now.

You may not be able to afford a **music supervisor**, but such a person advises you on your film's musical needs, negotiates the rights to prerecorded songs and supervises the composer. Often he is able to wangle great deals on music rights. Music supervisors exist in a fast-talking world between film and music, art and commerce. Make sure such a person puts your needs first.

COMPOSER

For the best possible musical score, hire a composer early (during preproduction, if possible). He will need a final edit of the film to time his compositions precisely, but he can get started with a script and your suggestions.

Just as dreamers create art, art begets dreamers. And just as thousands of starving artists call themselves actors or directors, there are similar numbers of composers out there. For this reason, you

157

probably won't have trouble finding someone with no scoring experience willing to labor for little or nothing. On the other hand, you may have trouble finding a talented composer who'll work within your meager budget. Give yourself time to search.

Composers can be found in the same manner as other production employees. The best methods are personal recommendations and via the screen credits of well-scored independent films and other low-budget productions. When you receive demo tapes, listen carefully to them. Does the music convey drama? Suspense? Romance? Does it avoid the clichéd sounds of cheap scores? Check all references. Is this person easy to work with? Does he come in on time and on budget? Make sure you and your potential composer feel the same about the film's musical needs and the money involved. For those of you with little to spend, a prominent "Music by" credit is sometimes enough currency; of course, there are always profit points and that last resort—deferred payment.

Some larger independent films have enough money to hire an **orchestra** for a day or two of scoring. Your composer or music supervisor should be able to help you find an appropriate symphonic group. If this doesn't fit into your budget, you may be able to locate an amateur orchestra (like the one at your local high school) that is looking to acquire experience, but this likely will require a large investment of patience for less-than-stellar results.

Chances are, your composer will be working with a small group of musicians or he'll be alone, with an orchestra/rock band/all-purpose musical extravaganza called a **synthesizer**. Beware of cheesy synth music. However, do not have an irrational fear of electronic audio. Many composers working with modern technology can make music that is barely distinguishable from that created entirely by "real people" with "real instruments." Furthermore, some synthetic sounds give an odd, emotion-inducing quality that actual instruments can't duplicate.

The important thing is not how the music is made. Instead, you should worry about how talented the person is who is creating it and how well he can compose music to accentuate your story.

One of the first things you and the composer will do (perhaps joined by the producer and editor) is have a **spotting session**, during which you'll watch the film and note places for music. At this point, you should be aware of the emotional content of your film, but you also may be too close to focus clearly. Therefore, take advantage of the composer's fresh perspective.

When you've "locked the picture" (finished editing), every moment that requires music, no matter how small, will be timed out to one-hundredths of a second so that the music can be composed precisely to the film.

Give your composer the time to work alone. Creativity seldom flourishes with a critic peaking over an artist's shoulder. However, be sure to let him know what you want. Check in on him just enough to be sure that the score is meeting your needs. If it isn't, find yourself a new composer.

PRERECORDED SONGS

In addition to, or in place of, composed music you may choose to use prerecorded songs. The good news is that most songs, no matter how popular, are *free* for use in independent films . . . at least for awhile. Many companies will provide you with **nonprofit releases,** enabling you to use their songs in your film when it is screened at festivals or for distributors. This isn't done out of the goodness of their hearts. If your movie is sold to a distributor or whenever you show your movie for profit, you must then pay a proper royalty fee to the record company and/or publishers for their songs or excise them from the movie.

Note that popular tunes that play over the front and end credits can command more than $30,000. Most any song of note that is used anywhere in a motion picture will cost at least $10,000 in royalty fees. And the sky's the limit as to what companies and publishers can charge.

Be aware of the downside of this "free music:" Distributors may not want to cover the bill. Beyond the studios, only the biggest distribution companies will be able to afford a six-digit music invoice. It's a judgment call whether or not to use a prohibitively popular song. Don't be overly eager to fill every frame with a classic tune, but on the other hand, don't be terrified of any song that ever had radio play.

For now, if your dream film includes a few known songs, you should put them in so you can show your film at festivals and to distributors and have it seen the way you want it to be seen, even if the songs have to come out later. (It worked for Tarantino, whose *Reservoir Dogs* would not be the same without "Stuck in the Middle with You" and the other 1970s tunes that fill it from start to finish.) Temporarily gratis songs are one of the few perks of independent filmmaking.

Whether you're getting a nonprofit release or securing all the licenses, the paperwork will build up. You'll need to acquire both the **master rights** (which indicate a specific version of the song, sung by a particular artist on a particular record) and the **publishing rights** (which indicate the original lyrics and music regardless who sings it). Master rights are generally held by the company that made the recording; publishing rights are generally owned by a music publishing company or the writer. Complicating things, a single song sometimes has several writers, each with a different publishing company; you'll need to get permission from each of the writers. Ownership information can be obtained from one of two songwriter organizations: BMI (310-659-9109) or ASCAP (213-883-1000).

Whichever entity you contact, the legal department will want such pertinent data as how much of the song you'd like to use, in what context it will be heard and a synopsis or statement regarding the content of the film.

Sometimes, beyond nonprofit clearances, you can get all the rights to a song for free—forever. This can happen if the song is more than seventy-five years old or if the author has been dead for more than fifty years or if the U.S. copyright has not been renewed. It then will go into the **public domain** and is therefore yours for the taking (this scenario is true of all copyrighted material: books, films, plays, etc.). Mozart, George Gershwin, Robert Johnson—their compositions are in p.d., as are the works of Shakespeare, F. Scott Fitzgerald and D.W. Griffith. The catch for music is that while a seventy-five-year-old *song* is in public domain, *recordings* of this song are not unless they too are more than seventy-five years old. For example, you can use Gershwin's *Rhapsody in Blue* without asking or paying, but you'll need the rights to use the 1996 version recorded by, say, the Boston Symphony Orchestra.

Owners of large amounts of copyrighted material are fighting to add decades onto the current law. In the meantime, you may find an old disc (or a remastered CD of said disc) to serve your purposes. Alternatively, you can hire musicians to re-record public domain songs.

Another way to acquire all the rights to a song for little or no money is to find an upcoming band and/or a record company pushing a new act. The world is full of "just about to breakthrough" groups that will benefit by having their song(s) heard by thousands, perhaps millions, of moviegoers. Bands without recording contracts will often let you take your pick of their "catalog;" they might even record something new for you. When it comes to songs by unknowns, you can almost always get someone to give you something for free. Hopefully, everyone will benefit in the end.

Finally, there are libraries full of low-priced **canned music**. A lab may be able to put you in touch with a fully orchestrated score, for only a few hundred dollars. The first potential problem with this is the difficulty of making a paint-by-numbers score fit your carefully crafted work of art. A lack of specific cuing and an inconsistency in theme and musical thread can be boldly obvious on the big screen. Another problem is that many canned scores, songs and **"stingers"** (short bursts of music to punctuate action) have been heard before, and even if they haven't, they often sound familiar. In other words, many canned scores sound canned. Sometimes, with the help of a sound editor or music supervisor, you can find music that sounds (or is altered to sound) fresh. Other times, the generic qualities of canned music can be used for an ironic effect. But be careful. Bad music can instantly cheapen and taint an otherwise original motion picture.

For information on soundtrack recordings and musical money-making, see "DOMESTIC THEATRICAL: Miscellaneous Ancillary: Music."

20/SOUND EDITING

Today, audio tracks are usually edited on computers. A fairly decent sound edit can be achieved on a typical nonlinear picture editing system (for those of you on super-low budgets), but for best results, you should hire at least one sound editor and hand them a copy of your edited film (on video) and the audio masters.

A sound editing computer is called a **digital audio workstation** (DAW). Popular brands include *Digidesign*, *AVID* and *Timeline*. Once the audio tracks have been digitized, a DAW allows the editor to monitor graphic representations of all sounds on a computer screen, indicating where a sound begins and ends. With this visual help, the dialogue, effects and music can easily be pulled, inserted and manipulated.

As the technology for DAWs continues to improve, outdated audio editing systems can be purchased fairly inexpensively. Therefore, just about any mixer or audiophile with some extra cash can become a sound cutter. Beware! As with everything, make sure your good deal produces good results: be certain that both the editor and his system can meet all of your needs in a timely and efficient manner. Larger films have separate employees to cut dialogue, music and sound effects. On low-budget movies, all such duties are often performed by the same person.

Sound editing is one of the final places where the director can implant his creative vision on the film. Sounds can vividly express moods, emotions and settings; background effects can conjure the aura of expensive locations; words can be distorted to make the audience uneasy crickets can sooth nerves. Audio can tell us things that pictures can't. Utilize this versatile tool to its fullest.

DIALOGUE

The first thing your sound editor should do is "clean up" the dialogue track(s). Often this is done without watching the film's visuals, but by listening carefully for any imperfections. If the sound was recorded with multiple microphones, the channels can be heard one after the other, with the best track selected. Pops, clicks and other audio pollution (including cars, planes and director's instructions) can be excised as long as no one is speaking at that exact moment. The room tones and ambient noises that were recorded during production are now used to fill in blank spots and to mask unwanted sounds. Dialogue can be **equalized** (raised or lowered to attain the proper volume level throughout).

Even with computers, dialogue editing is often tedious. Because it usually does not require the director's constant input, let your sound editor work on the dialogue track(s) for a week. Then check in and make suggestions.

Some lines may need to be rerecorded. The process of inserting new dialogue is called **dubbing** (or **looping**). This will necessitate bringing the actors back. Larger indies with name performers will need to reserve funds for this purpose. If your film is of the micro-budget variety, plead with your actors to give you one more day . . . for the "good of the film."

For best results, dubbing should be done in a modern sound studio with **A.D.R.** (automatic dialogue recording) equipment. Be prepared: renting the space and hiring the technicians can be expensive. In a squeeze, you can dub lines anywhere with an audio recorder (DAT or DA-88 are best). During this process, the actor watches the section of film and says what he needs to say at the appropriate moment. Make him do it several times, as you'll want options in order to precisely sync voices with lips.

EFFECTS & MUSIC

Most sound editors, even those editing in their garages, have extensive effects libraries. Your average professional studio will seemingly have *everything*. And what the studio doesn't have, it can buy, borrow or Foley. (Although a sound editor may insert FX, the director will, as always, have the final say.)

Fill your tracks with appropriate noises. The lack of small sounds—the kind you may think are inconsequential—can, almost subliminally, make your film feel incomplete, sterile or amateurish. Effects editing is like composing: all noises have their own meaning. Melded together, they can suggest moods, emotions, people, places and things.

Foley is the process of creating an audio effect during post-production. Studio films and large independents hire Foley artists who perform such sounds as footsteps, creaking doors, crinkling paper, etc., on a special stage while watching the film projected on a screen. You may not be able to afford a Foley artist, a special stage or a big screen, but no matter how over-budget you've gone, you can certainly find some shoes, doors and paper. Anyone with an audio recorder can create such common effects.

By this point, you and the composer have sweated over the music. Now it's a matter of fitting every note of the score and every prerecorded song into the exact spot in the highest quality condition. For the best audio, music should be in a digital format before it is transferred to a DAW. It is crucial that the accents of the composed score and all prerecorded songs precisely match your film's action. Make sure it's perfect.

MIX

Sound mixing is a big deal, usually requiring an established (i.e., expensive) facility, a team of technicians and several days. If you have the funds to make a completed answer print at this point, bite the bullet and use an experienced mixing studio to do your audio correctly. However, many of you will not be mixing for the big screen yet. Assuming you edited on a nonlinear system, you're still dealing with a video version of your film. You might not need a theatrical mix for some time, so you can save cash now by doing a preliminary mix. Minimum mixing ingredients include, a mixing board, a professional DAT or DA-88 recorder that allows you to "punch in" (seamlessly record from any spot on the tape) and, in addition to yourself, at least two people—one mixing, one recording.

In the beginning, the audio will be on numerous tracks for dialogue, effects and music. These can be raised, lowered or altered in subtle ways as they're brought together to form the soundtrack. Your job, as director, is to watch the film and to listen to the sound very carefully. Whenever something doesn't sound perfect or if you want to try it another way, speak up. Mix the tracks until all ingredients come together and produce precisely the sound you desire.

For clarity, only one sound element should dominate at any one time; to express a hectic pace, several can compete for attention. Remember: even the smallest sounds can make a difference. As always, keep the story and your overall vision paramount.

For all processes from the mixing stage onward, your audio should be **three-stripe**: one stripe (channel) is dialogue; another is music; the third is effects. This is important because it allows you to separate them later and give just the music and effects tracks (**M & E**) to an overseas distributor who will make a dub version by inserting a foreign language translation of your dialogue. This bastardizing process is, unfortunately, a necessity for most overseas sales.

A video **layback** session, in which sound is married to the picture, can usually be done by the sound mixer/editor. He will need the appropriate equipment in order to sync without drifting your time-coded master tape to the mixed-down audio. (Any typical sound facility can do this with ease.) Be sure to watch this process: there is nothing more distracting than sound out of sync with

picture. See also: "LAB, PART 2: Sound Revisited."

21/STOP!

So, here you are. Assuming you edited on a nonlinear system, you should have a Beta-SP or 3/4" master with a mixed soundtrack. There are miles to go before you sleep, and yet you have something that resembles a completed film. Now is the time to evaluate your position and map out a strategy for crossing to the promised land.

THE ROAD FROM HERE
With your video master, you can make VHS and 3/4" copies; this can be done relatively cheaply at a dubbing house or video transfer lab. Or, if you have at least two good VCRs (including one in the format of your master) and some high-quality blank videotapes, you can do it yourself for nothing.

Armed with video copies, you can send your film anywhere. But, if you want your film to be seen on the big screen and your production is out of money, you will need to acquire **finishing funds**. To round up more money you can do any one of the following:

- A video version of your film can be screened at the IFFM (Independent Feature Film Market), held each September in New York City (see "PUBLICITY, PART 2: spreading the word, part 2."). This is done either to secure completion money (via investors), festival berths (thus, attracting investors) or, best of all, distribution. In the latter case, a company may buy all the rights or the rights for only one territory, but even a foreign TV deal can provide your film with enough cash to complete a 35mm print.

166

- You can deliver videos directly to people and companies with deep pockets, asking them to help complete your movie by coming onboard as investors (often taking a large chunk of your profits). Indie maven John Pierson is the best-known finishing fund investor and producer's rep, having shepherded such pictures as *She's Gotta Have It, Roger & Me* and *Clerks* to lucrative distribution deals.

- You can submit a video to film festivals (see "FESTIVALS") and hope for acceptance. (Many such events require that you enter via video.) If you get accepted by Sundance or Toronto, completion cash will probably find its way to your movie.

- You can rent a comfortable space and arrange a screening of your film on a big-screen TV. Invite interested parties, including investors, distributors and festival programmers to have a look.

- You can send video copies directly to distributors around the world. This is usually not the best strategy for your film, but several notable micro-budget success stories (including *The Brothers McMullen* and *El Mariachi*) were first viewed by companies on video.

With video copies, you can do almost anything you can do with a film print to get finishing funds, distribution, festival berths and publicity. And you can do something you cannot do any other way: easily and cheaply show your dream film to a wide variety of people anywhere in the world.

But here's the bad news: videos have one great disadvantage which may outweigh all their benefits of mobility. The experience of watching a video on a TV screen does not and cannot compare to that of sitting in a dark theater surrounded by two dozen speakers and gazing at a sixty-foot screen. Therefore, your only chance at being selected for Sundance or getting picked up for distribution by Miramax may be shot because the executive's first impression of your comedy was not of it being projected in all its glorious color and mixed sound in a palace filled with enthusiastic laughter, but rather, on a small TV with a single speaker in a bright office, being paused every few minutes to take a call.

So what's your best strategy for distribution? As with so much in the world of nonstudio entertainment, your film's course will be set primarily by your cash flow.

If you shot on 35mm and you have the money to finish a 35mm print, by all means do it. That said, if you're disappointed by what you've created, you could get tapes to a few festivals or advisors (but not distributors). If the verdict is wholly negative, you can save cash by stepping on the brakes and pursuing a more cautious video strategy. But let's not think negatively. Assuming you're charging forward to a 35mm answer print, don't let anyone else but yourself and any other producer(s) take a video copy home. You don't want a small-screen version leaking out before you unveil the big-screen product.

If you shot on Super 16 and have enough money to make a Super 16 print but not a 35mm blow-up, this is an easy call: don't make the print. For now, get it on the best video format possible, since you probably won't be able to screen Super 16 outside of the lab anyway. Conceivably, you could make a Super 16 print and invite investors, festival directors and distributors to the lab for a screening, but this may be a lot of trouble and money for nothing; most industry people will probably just say "send a video."

If you shot on 16mm and have enough cash to make a 16mm print but not a 35mm blow-up, you probably should make the print. Making a 16mm print is not horribly expensive (around $15,000, including white-on-black titles, negative cut, optical track and answer print) and regular 16mm projectors are common. With a print, you can show your motion picture on big screens at markets and festivals as well as privately for investors and distributors.

If you don't have the money for a print on any stock, then your decision is simple: you'll have to stop and raise funds. This probably will entail sending VHS copies to potential investors, screening your film on video as a "work-in-progress" at IFFM, submitting videos to festivals and generally trying to create a positive buzz.

Sending a tape directly to acquisition executives at distribution companies around the world is a trickier matter because this is basically your last chance (and not a very good one). But if you have exhausted all investor possibilities, it may be time to start working the phones and shipping out videos. Consider a few European release companies and broadcasters first; such a sale won't make you rich but it can provide you with enough cash to finish your film on 35mm.

More about distribution is found in the aptly titled "DISTRIBUTION" section.

For those of you not yet making a print, you may want to skip ahead, as the search for a release company to market your vision will now supersede the techniques of filmmaking and become your overriding passion.

22/LAB, PART 2

Hopefully, you've been doing things right so far. This is especially true if you have a budget of less than $200,000. The amount of money needed to get a micro-budget film through the final stretch and over the finish line can easily supersede all money spent so far, and this is compounded if the sound and picture editing must be redone to make a commercial-quality print. Even if a distributor is paying for your finishing costs, this money invariably will be subtracted from your profits (if any).

SOUND REVISITED
The audio hopefully will sound passable on your video masters. However, today's standards for theatrical sound are so great that your local multiplex can quickly make the best efforts of low-budget editors and mixers sound hollow and amateurish. Major distributors who purchase micro-budget films have been known to spend more than $150,000 to reedit and remix soundtracks for theaters.

A second swipe at sound editing could mean a major overhaul. You may have to go back to the original recordings and reconstruct the tracks; you may have to "clean up" and enhance your tracks; it may mean new songs or a new composed score; it could mean improved sound effects or better A.D.R.; perhaps you'll have to schedule a more technologically advanced mixing session. If you got it right the first time, it could mean no extra work at all. Under all circumstances, maintain control of your picture. Do not sign away final cut (picture or audio) to a distributor.

Once you're satisfied with the edit and mix, it's time to make a track for the big screen and big speakers. You'll need a three-stripe

optical soundtrack that can be joined to the film and projected. Your mixed master tape is transferred to magnetic film, the magnetic signal of which is then translated into an optical signal for an optical master track; this, in turn, is printed onto the edge of your film. Don't worry about the details. Lab technicians do this technical work; just make sure it sounds perfect.

TITLES & OPTICALS
A title house or an optical facility with a titles department can do the film's main titles (found in the front of the movie) and rear titles (found in the credit crawl at the back of the film). White titles on black background are not a major expense (about $2,000 or so); on the other hand, elaborate visuals can cost more than the entire budget of an independent film.

Optical effects other than basic titles, such as fades, slow-motion, freezes, split-screens and superimposed titles, are potentially budget-busting expenses. Avoid writing opticals into your shooting script in the first place. But, if they're in the script and money becomes tight, try to write them out. If you must have an optical effect, you won't have much room for negotiation: this is a terrible category for bargain-shopping.

When selecting a lab to create your optical effects, choose one with a stellar reputation because technicians will be working with your original, highly scratchable negative. Damage to the negative is almost always irreversible, so even a tiny scratch will be an eternal scar.

NEGATIVE CUTTING
Assuming you have edited your film on a nonlinear system, the computer will print out a list of your cuts. If you edited in a linear or "old school" method, this list will be generated by a person with a pencil and a log sheet who makes careful notations while reading the edge numbers on a video monitor (linear) or on strips of film ("old-school"). You'll then give this list to the lab and the negative cutter will slice and splice your original camera negative to match your list. Such a service will cost a few thousand dollars.

Warning: Make sure you're completely happy with every frame of your film before the cutter begins assembling the negative. Any changes after the negative is cut will be very expensive.

PRINTS

A crucial component of print-making is **timing**; this is when computers shade and color-correct the negative. At the lab, during timing, the cinematographer (alone or with you) supervises the footage as it is printed "up" (made lighter) or printed "down" (made darker). Specific colors can be intensified or diminished.

It's time for the lab to make a first trial composite **answer print**. This should be screened by the cinematographer, director and the lab's timer. Color and density corrections can still be made at this point.

Depending on the film format and how many corrections are done, an answer print can cost between $5,000 and $20,000. When it's completed, you'll have a film capable of being screened. (But, of course, if your answer print is Super 16, you probably won't be able to screen it outside of the lab.)

If you shot your film 16mm or Super 16, you'll eventually want to get your answer print blown up to 35mm. The price for this will be at least $40,000. Chances are, you won't have the money for this (if you had it, you probably would have shot your movie in 35mm in the first place). But if you manage to come up with finishing funds, use only a lab that has lots of experience at blowing up prints (such as DuArt). The quality of this process will be crucial, as virtually everyone who views your film will see it after it has optically doubled in size.

Unless you distribute the film yourself, release prints will be handled by the distributor. Assuming the distributor releases more than a handful of prints at a time, the company won't jeopardize the original negative by putting its highly scratchable surface through the rigors of print-making. Therefore, an **internegative** (additional negative) will be made. To get the internegative, a lab will first need to strike an **interpositive** and then make a **check print** to evaluate how the internegative looks. (All three of these together will typically cost more than $25,000.)

Release prints are made from the internegative. Prints are one of the largest expenses of distribution, typically costing more than $2,000 apiece, plus the cost of fresh internegatives on occasion. Added to this is the cost of sending 35mm prints to theaters across the country or around the world. You can see why it's a big deal for an indie to get onto even one-hundred screens simultaneously. Because of print-making, distribution and advertising costs, many small art films never play at more than six theaters at a time.

DISTRIBUTION

23/PUBLICITY, PART 2

Remember that mantra about film being a marketing industry. It will never be as true as it is now, when you're looking for a distributor for your film. Begin by honing a three-sentence pitch for your movie. It's also useful at this juncture to have a unique way of attracting attention to your production. Independent filmmakers are expected to have interesting war stories.

Find a production **hook**: run-ins with the law, catastrophes or near-catastrophes, actors with amnesia, turtles eating camera cables, shooting scripts spontaneously combusting . . . some sort of miracle or mayhem. If no compelling anecdote comes to mind, make something up. Hint: Your slim budget isn't all that fascinating anymore. *El Mariachi* and *Clerks* lowered that bar so far that if you now claim to have made a flick for twenty grand nobody bats an eye. Come up with something that sells. When in doubt, stick to the classics: sex and violence. Film is a marketing industry.

PRESS KITS

One of the most important things for post-production publicity is a press kit. This will consist of cast and crew credits, a synopsis (one to two pages), production notes (two to three pages of interesting information on making the movie) and brief biographies of key cast and crew people (especially those who have notable resumés). Print it with laser-quality type, double-spaced, on 24-lb. paper, with a cover page. You can make an even greater impression by placing your press kit into a glossy folder with the film's title printed on the cover and enclosing three to five 8x10 production stills.

When your movie gets distributed, the official press kit may also include such items as the key art (original advertising), positive reviews (and quotes from critics) and previously published feature stories about your movie. With theatrical distribution, there may also be an electronic press kit (EPK) for television and/or radio use (see "marketing").

SPREADING THE WORD, PART 2

Press kits are announcements. They can be sent directly to acquisition executives at distribution companies. They can be mailed to magazines aimed at the indie cinema market, such as *Filmmaker, Film Comment, MovieMaker* and *The Independent Film and Video Monthly*. For fantasy, science fiction and horror movies, major publications include *Cinefantastique, Starlog* and *Fangoria*. Press kits can be sent to film critics. They can also be delivered to local newspapers, radio programs and festival committees. They can be posted on the Internet. They can be given to anyone who may be able to help your film or your career. Start by asking your own cast and crew for suggestions: if half the folks on your payroll have one significant contact in entertainment, news or publishing, that's a lot of people who should know about your movie.

It won't hurt to spread the news to celebrities—those influential people in various walks of life (arts, politics, media, sports) whose opinions are valued by the media. If Michael Crichton or Michael Jordan praises your little film, it could start a positive chain reaction. Send press kits, letters and/or videos. Invite celebrities to screenings. Utilize all the connections you can.

In addition to negotiating the eventual deal, an **agent, manager** or **producer's rep** can help spread the word. Agents typically take ten percent off the top of any sale; managers and producer's reps (usually lawyers) typically take more. No one gets paid unless you do, so convincing someone to represent your work is half the battle. Before signing with a representative, make certain he will push your film tirelessly and he won't lose interest if the initial response is lukewarm. Also, be sure he has good connections in the industry and a thorough knowledge of distribution. As a function of their jobs, representatives often attend film markets and festivals around the world, so they can spread the word in such faraway places as Milan, Berlin and Cannes—places you probably couldn't afford to go on your own. If you don't get representation now, you should obtain it before negotiating any deal.

Another key method for spreading the word (and, as mentioned earlier, perhaps the best way to find finishing funds) is to attend the **Independent Feature Film Market** (IFFM), held each September at the Angelika Film Center in New York City. Born in 1979, it is the only market in the world devoted exclusively to American independent films (narrative features, shorts and documentaries). The annual deadline for submissions is in June. A motion picture may be submitted as a completed work (in 16mm, 35mm and video), as a work-in-progress or as a screenplay seeking financing. Entry fees are several hundred dollars per category. For more information, contact IFP/East in New York.

If you are going to the IFFM, contact major buyers <u>before</u> you arrive so they know who you are and what you are selling. Pique their interest: give them just enough info so they can't afford to miss your creation. Write an outstanding synopsis for the market's catalogue because it could be read by an acquisition executive at every distribution company in America and many around the world. The catalogue also will be handed out at most of our planet's best film festivals.

Upon arriving, be prepared with business cards, press kits and your pitch. Be professional as you create a buzz for your film. Know that not many deals are closed at IFFM but many begin there.

If you have a very good movie (whether or not it has a distribution deal), you may be able to get it screened as part of the New Directors/New Films series held each April at the Museum of Modern Art in New York City. This forum has been a launching pad for several independent features and directors. Press and industry attention is great; so is the competition for admittance.

The screening series of IFP/West in Los Angeles, called "Director's Cut," and IFP/East in New York, called "Independents Night" are not as prestigious but they are easier to get into. Other organizations hold similar events throughout the year. If your film is accepted to one, spread the word! Send invitations to acquisition execs, studio development folks and the local press.

Make sure you're well-prepared before attending any festival at which your film is screening (see "FESTIVALS" for more on this). Let distributors and the press know about your work before arriving. When you get there, "work" the conferences and parties (avoid drinking on the job) to bring as many people as possible into a screening of your film. Because personal impressions and reputations are of great importance (factoring into awards, reviews and sales), be extra polite to everyone.

One crucial feature of film festivals, markets and other screenings is getting your film reviewed. Independent films, with their art house audience, almost always sink or swim on the strength of **reviews**. Be polite to critics; be happy that your little picture is being reviewed at all. But there's not much you can do. Either they'll like it or they won't. If anything positive is said, play it up and then some. If reviews are negative, try to learn from them; then forget about 'em.

And finally, be sure to follow through once the festival is over. Buyers, investors and the press get swamped at film fests and markets: there's so much to see, so many people to meet, so many things to consider. Therefore, write or call a week or two after the event. Remind them who you are and ask what they thought of your film. Even if they think your dream project should be sliced into guitar picks, it's best to know where you stand.

MARKETING

When your film obtains theatrical distribution, marketing will be a crucial component in its box-office performance. At this point, spreading the word will come at the distributor's expense, but you still will be responsible for much of it.

The distributor will take virtually everything from your production that is capable of generating publicity: photos, press books, biographies, artwork, behind-the-scenes footage and outtakes, sometimes even props and costumes. Slides or contact sheets of your stills are especially important. They'll make **selects** of the image(s) they feel will best sell your movie. You may not have a say in this. Their favorite image may pop up everywhere—in magazines and newspapers. And, foreign territories will likely follow suit. Next year, one of the shots your cousin Pete snapped may be on billboards from New Orleans to New Guinea.

A **one-sheet** poster will be designed. The importance of this cannot be underestimated because it sets in stone the most identifiable single image of your motion picture and it is usually the nexus for all other visual ads. Independent film posters often include favorable quotes from critics (who by now have had a sneak preview of it) or listings of any festival awards.

Newspaper ads are a must. Theatrical exhibitors absorb much of the huge expense of placing ads in the newspapers. In order to build interest, the largest ads generally appear during the week before and the first two weeks of the movie's release. Although large dailies give the most exposure, they can be prohibitively expensive; alternative weekly papers are considered good venues for indies as they address a young, trendy, open-minded audience. Your small independent film may not warrant the expense of **magazine ads** (which are usually full page and in color); furthermore, the national scope of most major magazines is probably unsuitable for the limited release of your independent film. That said, magazine ads can be used effectively to target specialized films to specialized audiences via specialized publications (race, hobby, etc.).

The distributor will also make a **trailer** (popularly known as a "preview" or "coming attraction"), to be shown before another film. Trailers are two or three minutes long and usually present highlights in a compelling, manipulative fashion. They are especially important to on indie because your movie probably won't have many (if any) television commercials or talk show opportunities. In addition, because trailers for indies often run before other indies, your picture is advertising directly to its targeted audience. As with most components in the marketing campaign, you may have no say about this crucial mini-movie.

The trailer may form the backbone of an **electronic press kit.** This is a video or audio version of the written press kit, containing clips designed to make an immediate impact; it is distributed to television or radio programs. The EPK can also include interviews with you and members of the cast and crew. Studios commonly produce EPKs for their films, but since your electronic media exposure may be slim, your distributor may not bother. Similarly, national **TV advertising** may be out of your release company's budget; any such ads probably will be run on specialized cable channels.

More common for independent films are **radio ads**. Usually created in lengths of thirty or sixty seconds, these spots should offer the flavor of your movie—in audio. Sometimes, sound bites from the movie are included. Radio spots are much cheaper than TV advertising and can be targeted more directly. Over-the-radio **ticket giveaways** are sometimes done in conjunction with or in lieu of radio spots.

When your movie is released, reviews will continue to be a crucial barometer of success. After word-of-mouth, critical press is your cheapest and best avenue for publicity. Viewers who regularly see non-studio films are usually more discerning than the typical action and slapstick fans. They actually read reviews. The right critical response can make you; the wrong one can break you.

There are multitudes of other ways to advertise and market a film: **the Internet, billboards, direct mail, flyers, promotional appearances, product giveaways** . . . limited only by you and your distributor's imagination. Do not depend on your distributor to do everything. Money could be tight. As long as your activities don't run counter to the larger campaign, do what you can to market your movie. Post flyers on bulletin boards (coffee houses, colleges, laundromats . . .) and plaster one-sheets on construction site board-ups (where legal, of course). Get on the Internet. Wear a shirt, hat or jacket with your movie's name on it everywhere you go and get others to do the same. Spread the word.

Mostly what promoting an independent film boils down to is you, the director/producer. You're the best advertisement for your creation. As your movie opens in various cities, the distributor may fly you around with it. If not, you'll be spending lots of time on the phone. Bigger distributors will have a **publicity agent** to arrange various print, radio, television and Internet interviews. Be humble and have a story to tell. People will want to hear something compelling about the making of your movie. The more interesting you are, the more interviews you'll do (sometimes accompanied by one of your actors or a recognizable crew member), the more free advertising you'll get.

You'll get sick of saying the same thing over and over again (try to come up with fresh angles—reporters want "news"). You'll get sick of college towns. You'll get sick of every frame of a movie you started more than two years earlier and now seem to be tethered to. But then you'll realize how incredibly hard you worked to get to this place and how amazingly lucky you are to be here and how many other people worked just as hard but weren't as lucky, and you'll slap yourself and get well fast. Filmmaking is a marketing industry.

24/FESTIVALS

Festivals are the engines that drive the independent film train. Several scenarios exist for your film if it is festival-bound:

- If you have an unfinished film and you get into a major festival, a distributor may take an advance look, buy the distribution rights and provide finishing funds as part of the purchasing price.

- If your movie is completed, it can be picked up for distribution at a festival.

- If your film already has a distributor, it could be entered for the publicity value.

- Or, in the most common occurrence, your motion picture is presented in a festival and it is the only place it is ever publicly seen.

Festivals are the one constant. They're where you and your movie are introduced to the press, the distributors, the studios and the core audience. A film festival may well be the launching pad for your motion picture and your career.

MAJOR FESTS

The U.S. Film Festival began in 1978; it was taken over by Robert Redford in 1985 and rechristened **The Sundance Film Festival.** It has been the preeminent event for American independent cinema since the late 1980s. After making a quality movie, getting invited to "the 'dance" is the single most important factor in obtaining a distribution deal. It's held for ten days each January in Park City, Utah.

Sundance has two categories for narrative films: the Dramatic Competition (eighteen films compete for awards) and the American Spectrum (eighteen films by first-time directors are screened but do not compete). There's also the Frontier Section (more experimental work), a short film competition and a documentary competition. Foreign indies and some higher-profile American efforts are shown out of competition.

Theaters and hotel rooms are scarce and some feel that Sundance went "Hollywood" years ago and now attracts too many studio weasels. Still, this remains the most influential indie fest in the world. Competition for admittance is very stiff: more than 800 narrative feature submissions were received for 1998 (up from a mere sixty in 1987). The entry fee is minimal.

Aside from Sundance, there are a few other international film festivals of large magnitude. The biggest are listed below, in chronological order:

The Rotterdam International Film Festival (The Netherlands, February) competes for prestige with the European "Big Three" that follow it on the calendar. Begun in 1971, Rotterdam lately has been accepting more American independents, scouting for them at the IFFM and Toronto fest (Sundance comes after Rotterdam's entry deadline).

The Berlin International Film Festival (Germany, February) was established in West Berlin in 1950 as an Allied cultural pageant and has been one of the premiere film fests for decades. Traditionally Eurocentric (and associated with gay and avant-garde cinema), Berlin, like Rotterdam, has increased its selection of U.S. indies in recent years, occasionally selecting films that don't make the cut at Sundance. There are four categories, all of which accept American entries: the Main Competition, an International Forum, the "Panorama" Section for more experimental work and a film market.

Cannes Film Festival (France, May) is the king of all film extravaganzas. It was founded in 1946, and has been annual since 1949. Cannes is a film market and "event" more than it is a competitive film festival, even though its jury prizes still carry great prestige. Cannes accepts only a select few American independents for competition, occasionally of the low-budget variety. Filmmakers whose movies are not invited to compete but who are seeking worldwide distribution and who are willing to absorb the large travel and entry expenses can screen their work in the popular Market Section.

Venice Film Festival (Italy, September) began in 1931. This was the world's first true film festival and is another giant international extravaganza. Like Cannes, it's an event more than a competition. Many of its American films are multi-million dollar mainstream studio efforts. It accepts only a few U.S. indies but sometimes its selections have been overlooked by other festivals.

The Toronto International Film Festival (Canada, September) is your best bet if you want to screen your motion picture in a foreign festival; and not just because it offers the shortest plane flight. This cinema bonanza—begun in 1975—may outweigh Sundance as North America's finest seller's market. Hordes of industry execs, sales agents and reporters descend on Ontario each autumn. Along with movies from around the world, it accepts a healthy cross-section of U.S. indies, including micro-budget fare. Getting into Toronto is a big boost towards acceptance at Sundance; and chances are good that you'll then go on to the 'dance with a distributor in tow. Conversely, if you don't make it into Sundance, the odds are slim of being accepted to Toronto the following fall.

The New York Film Festival (September/October) was founded in 1962. This venerable non-competitive showcase immediately follows Toronto and comes only a few weeks after IFFM. It exhibits films from around the world, including a few of the best American independents. Entry competition is stiff (in 1996, it selected twenty-nine moction pictures from a total of 1,400 entries). Its greatest strength is that it brings films to the attention of the influential New York media. Classy and somewhat aloof, the New York Film Festival holds itself above the frenzy of markets and competitions, therefore, it's not exactly a seller's bonanza. But it is truly a prestigious showcase for your work.

Most of the major festivals have entry fees. As previously mentioned, it works to your advantage to screen a print for a selection committee (often, selectors for one festival will see your film at another), but you also can submit your film on videotape (3/4" format is best). Some competitions require that you only submit on video.

Getting into Sundance should be your primary goal. Like all festivals, Sundance likes to premiere films. Submissions must not have played any previous U.S. festivals and can only have screened at a maximum of two foreign fests.

Try and get your film accepted to Toronto (a foreign fest) and follow that with the IFFM. Endeavor to get someone on the selection committee of Sundance to see your film with an audience at either one of these events. Hopefully, the Sundance selection committee will accept your film right then and there.

If your film doesn't show publicly, try to set up a screening for someone on the Sundance selection committee. If you don't have a completed print (on 16mm or 35mm), you can wait until next year while trying to raise completion funds or you can submit a 3/4" videotape. Then, polish your rabbit's foot and pray.

THE REST OF THE FESTS

For the majority of you who won't have your rabbit's foot or prayers answered and who aren't accepted into one of the major festivals listed above, cheer up. First, know that you're in good company. In 1992, Carl Franklin's superb film, *One False Move* (written by and featuring Billy Bob Thornton), was rejected by Sundance and every other festival it was submitted to. It was nevertheless picked up for distribution by I.R.S. Releasing and went on to critical accolades and financial success. (Siskel and Ebert both proclaimed it the best film of the year.) Also, assuming you have a finished 16mm or 35mm print, there still are a few hundred lesser-known showcases to choose from, many of which are begging for full-length features.

Throughout the world, several small film festivals are scheduled each week. The more respected of these (listed chronologically) include:

The Slamdance Film Festival (Utah, January) began in 1995 by three filmmakers whose movies were rejected by Sundance. This feisty festival has been run near and at the same time as Sundance, thus stirring up attention. What started as a guerilla-fest quickly became respectable. For 1998, there were more than 1,700 submissions for its forty slots (twenty for features, twenty for shorts). Slamdance has quickly become a viable sock hop for those spurned by Sundance's more polished waltz. First films are shown in competition.

185

The **Los Angeles Independent Film Festival** (April) was inaugurated in 1995 and immediately acquired player status by virtue of its location in the middle of "the industry." A relatively high percentage of movies have been picked up for distribution here. In 1997, the festival received more than 1,000 submissions and selected twenty-two features and twenty-four shorts. LAIFF is a good second showcase for films which have played at Sundance or Slamdance or a fine introduction for Utah rejects.

The **Taos Talking Pictures Festival** (New Mexico, April) is a respectable little show in a beautiful location and it is very supportive of independents. Currently, the prize for the feature film "Innovation Award" is five acres of land in Taos.

Established in 1975, the **Seattle Film Festival** (May-June) has a strong reputation for being genuinely independent and for introducing new talent. Spread over three weeks, this event is traditionally receptive to unique productions. As with alternative music in the early 1990s, Seattle is now host to a burgeoning alternative film scene, and that has fueled a great deal of interest in this venue.

The **Florida Film Festival** (near Orlando, June) started in 1992. This small fest has been achieving clout in recent years, due partly to increased film production and industry attention in the region.

The **Montreal World Film Festival** (August) begun in 1977 and remains the largest, truly *international* cinematic festival in North America, although its prestige has slipped in recent years. Few U.S. indies make it into competition here, but many are selected for the non-award categories. (Some feel this French-speaking venue is less than receptive to English language films.)

The **Telluride Film Festival** (August) was started in 1973 and has a respected tradition for putting filmmakers first. This Colorado fest offers a consistently dignified (if not particularly daring) showcase in a delightful vacation locale and receives considerable industry attention. This is a good place to get noticed.

The **Hamptons International Film Festival** (October) was reincarnated in 1994. Held in a tony Long Island community, this competition receives significant New York press.

For gay-themed films, the majors come one after the other: the **New York Lesbian & Gay Film Festival** (June), the **San Francisco International Lesbian and Gay Film Festival** (June) and **Outfest: The Los Angeles Gay & Lesbian Film Festival** (July). All receive considerable attention in the local and national gay press. Additionally, after the success of lesbian-themed indies such as *Go Fish* and *The Incredibly True Adventures of Two Girls in Love*, distributors, studios and mainstream publications are well-represented at these festivals.

There are many more film festivals. Most major (and a lot of minor) cities have one. Find out their basic requirements. Many do not accept American independents. Instead, they focus on foreign films, retrospective showings of classic or neglected works, or on experimental media. The City by the Bay, for example, has been holding the venerable **San Francisco International Film Fesival** for more than forty years; it's the oldest movie fest in the Western Hemisphere. It typically screens more than two hundred movies from more than fifty countries, but because of its worldwide diversity it has very little space for American independents. **London, Edinburgh,** and **Tokyo** are other important international fests that admit few, if any, U.S. indies.

Still, there are plenty of other festivals eager for your work. Many openly advertise for submissions. The fact is there's no shortage of communities that would love to experience a fraction of the worldwide attention and piles of cash that Sundance generates for Park City, Utah (population: 3,000) each year. Austin has two respectable fests: the (South by Southwest) **SXSW Film Festival & Conference** (March) and the **Heart of Film Festival** (October). **Ft. Lauderdale** (November) and **Honolulu** (November) are among the cities with state-of-the-art international showcases that welcome U.S. independents. There are better-than-average fests everywhere, and new ones are launching all the time.

One of your principal considerations in choosing a film festival is the cost involved:

- There will be an entry fee.

- You'll need to make a second print ($2,000) or screen your answer print (risky).

- You'll have to ship your film insured and/or travel to the festival and stay in a hotel.

And what does this get you? Perhaps an award. (Festivals hand out lots of awards.) Although grand prize cash could pay your rent, most accolades are little more than a trophy. You may get reviewed in the local press (and, in Los Angeles and New York, the local press has tremendous industry clout) or you may get a mention in a national publication. And maybe, just maybe, if you win a prize and collect some rave reviews, an acquisition exec will smile on your movie and you'll get a distribution deal.

But it's a long shot. Winning prizes or creating a buzz at a regional showcase may feed your ego and rekindle your dreams, but it's certainly no guarantee that distributors will notice, let alone open their checkbooks.

By all means, enter your film in festivals, but do so not with delusions of mega-success but with a clear head and a professional strategy. If you fail to get into Sundance or Toronto or New York, don't despair. Instead, select a few festivals that are more popular and influential than others or select those which are located near your home, thus enabling you to cut down on travel expenses and to maximize turnout and press attention.

When a festival asks, deliver an up-to-date, well-written, professional press kit with information on you, your film and the people involved in it, along with your best production stills. This is very important: such information often goes unedited into festival guides and local newspapers and it can make a huge initial impression on potential viewers (including critics and buyers). If possible, negotiate a favorable screening time (weekend evenings are best).

Work the event with business cards, press kits, your short pitch and a perpetually friendly, positive attitude. Remember: connections can lead to a distribution deal but, they can also lead to future financing or other career opportunities. Think of a film festival as an extended job interview . . . with popcorn. And try to have fun.

25/DOMESTIC THEATRICAL

We've already discussed how best to reach acquisition executives at distribution companies, but let's review:

- Work the press.

- Create a buzz.

- Keep your pitch simple.

- If possible, show your movie to distributors on a big screen at a festival (Sundance and Toronto are the best) or at the IFFM.

- If festival play is not possible, arrange screenings for execs; never send videos if you have a print. (On the other hand, if you don't have a print and you have no prospects of obtaining financing for one, call distributors, whet their appetites and ship them a high-quality video.)

It's an accepted rule that you should never show a rough cut to distributors. (In this case, a "rough cut" is a film which has not been completely edited; this is different from a "work-in-progress" which is edited but needs a 35mm blow-up and, perhaps, better audio.) But even this good advice has been shattered successfully. MGM/UA bought *Leaving Las Vegas* after some assembled footage was viewed on a nonlinear computer; Miramax first saw *Squeeze* on an Avid before snatching it up; and Miramax bought *Fresh* on the basis of its dailies!

Timing is crucial. Strike while your film is hot, not lukewarm (it sometimes takes time to build the heat), and certainly before it begins cooling (it can go ice cold in a hurry). Take the case of Alexander Rockwell's *In the Soup*. It won the Grand Jury Prize at Sundance (1992); independent distributors were clamoring for it. A dream come true, right? Unfortunately, the producers convinced themselves they could get a studio deal and they used their valuable but limited "hot time" shopping their bizarre, black-and-white art flick to the Hollywood majors. The big boys didn't bite. The *Soup* went cold and lost its flavor. Worst yet, when they returned to the indies, those companies had moved on to other food. *In the Soup* was ladled to tiny Triton Pictures (since deceased) for no advance. To get even the smallest theatrical release, the producers had to pay for prints and advertising themselves.

Learn from this monumental blunder. You're only the next big thing until the next, next big thing, and it's always right around the corner and closing fast. They call hot Hollywood properties "flavor of the month," but you probably won't get thirty days. At a major festival, your fortunes can rise and fall within twenty-four hours. Get hot and get signed.

THE COMPANIES
In the late 1980s, independent film distribution was dominated by such companies as Island, Vestron, Avenue and Cinecom. By the beginning of the 1990s, overextended and hammered by a few flops, these companies were out of business. Meanwhile, current heavyweights like October, Sony Pictures Classics and Fox Searchlight weren't born until the early-to mid-1990s. Independent distribution is in a constant state of flux. One distributor drops a few bombs and files for bankruptcy. Another gets absorbed by a studio and goes on a shopping spree.

Before screening your film for buyers, check on the current state of the distribution business (if you have an agent, manager or producer's rep, this will be his job). You don't want to be tied to a company spiraling downward; your dream project could get tangled in legal tape and never get released.

Shopping your motion picture and signing a deal should always have an ultimate goal: getting the widest possible distribution for your film. (This is not necessarily the same as getting the most money—at least, not in the short term.) Your goal should be to attain a significant domestic theatrical release (meaning the U.S. and

Canada) and your odds of getting this will be strongest if you go with the healthiest, hardest-working company.

Hollywood studios are the world's largest movie dispensers, filling projectors everywhere with a continuously flowing stream of entertainment. They generate their own product; they don't need what you make. Still, sometimes they can't resist. On occasion, the majors will pick up an independent film.

In the late 1980s, **Warner Bros.** released *Roger & Me* (for which they paid $3 million) and *Stand and Deliver* (for which they paid $5 million). In the 1990s, **Columbia** picked up *El Mariachi* and *Get On the Bus*, while **TriStar**, its sister studio, fell for *If Lucy Fell*. **MGM/ UA** recently drank to *Leaving Las Vegas*, following it with the chasers *It's My Party* and *Hurricane Streets*. **Paramount** served up *Kiss Me, Guideo*. The major studios will buy an indie, but they're not usually active shoppers. Feel free to approach them but your best realistic scenario is to sell to a major indie.

There are currently six independent film companies which are considered **major indies**. These six are in a position to cut you a solid deal and to get your movie into wide release (by non-studio standards): two hundred or more screens simultaneously. The major indies are (in alphabetical order):

Fine Line Features was born in 1991 and is the artistic sister of the larger, more mainstream indie studio **New Line Cinema** (which produced such films as *Seven* and *Dumb and Dumber*). Fine Line was one of the original indie outlaws; it was founded in 1967, by current CEO Bob Shaye and was built on a foundation of *Pink Flamingos* and similar midnight movies. New Line and Fine Line share Los Angeles offices and personnel. The companies were bought in 1994 by Ted Turner (whose company then merged with the even-more-massive Time-Warner). Fine Line released eight pictures in 1996, including the Oscar-winning hit *Shine*. Other titles in its library include *Hoop Dreams, The Player, My Own Private Idaho, House Party* and *Crash*.

Fox Searchlight (Los Angeles, CA) is the offspring of major studio Twentieth Century Fox. It made a big splash with its first pickup, *The Brothers McMullen*, in 1995. It also acquired 1997's *The Full Monty* and *Star Maps*. Produced films includes: *Girl 6, Stealing Beauty* and *She's the One*.

191

Gramercy (Beverly Hills, CA) is owned by international media giant PolyGram. This is a major indie producer but it has only recently become an active buyer with the British pick-up *Shallow Grave* and the American-made *When We Were Kings* and *Going All the Way*. Its impressive list of produced films includes: *Dead Man Walking, Four Weddings and a Funeral, The Usual Suspects* and *Fargo*.

Miramax (New York, NY) is chaired by brothers Harvey and Bob Weinstein in a hands-on manner. This once-small company exploded with the success of *sex, lies, and videotape* in 1989. It has distributed many of the biggest independent hits of the 1990s (can you spell Tarantino?), and is famous for outbidding other distributors at Sundance. Bought by Disney in 1993, Miramax has since shelled out remarkable sums for its pickups, including $5 million for *Swingers* (which was made for $250,000) and $10 million for *Sling Blade* (which was made for $1.2 million). Miramax released more than thirty titles in 1996 and similar numbers in 1997. Its library includes *Pulp Fiction, Clerks, The Piano, The Crying Game, Trainspotting* and *The English Patient*.

October Films (Los Angeles), a young and aggressive buyer, was sold to Universal Pictures in 1997. October Films picks up several motion pictures each year for distribution (nine in 1996) and has a reputation for handling limited releases with care. Films in its library include *Ruby in Paradise, The Last Seduction* and *Lost Highway*. October ascended to a new level in early 1997, when two of its foreign pickups, *Secrets & Lies* and *Breaking the Waves*, received Academy Award nominations.

Sony Pictures Classics (Culver City, CA) is the arthouse arm of Sony Pictures Entertainment (which also owns major studios TriStar and Columbia). Sony Pictures Classics distributed fourteen films in 1996, including the indie hit *Lone Star*. This company has a reputation for developing gentel fare; its first release, in 1992, was *Howard's End*. Still, it's outbid other companies for some of the best in recent cutting-edge cinema. Sony Pictures Classics is notorious for careful, tight-fisted distribution strategies. Its library includes *SubUrbia, Mi Vida Loca, Crumb* and *Welcome to the Dollhouse*.

In addition to these major indies, there are **mini indies**—smaller companies with smaller bankrolls. Because they can provide hands-on care, they're often a better fit for certain niche films. Then again, they might not have the funds to get your dream project into enough theaters or to mount a proper marketing and publicity campaign.

Most are open to documentaries as well as to narrative features. The best of the minis include:

Arrow Entertainment (New York) was founded in 1993. This small company has released such movies as *My Life's in Turnaround, Combination Platter* and *Breathing Room.*

Castle Hill (New York), in business since 1978, is a company which distributes a diverse collection of old and new features (usually in a very limited way), including *Prayer of the Rollerboys* and the documentary *A Great Day in Harlem.*

CFP (Cinepix Film Properties; New York, NY) is also known as Cinepix. This Canadian company bankrolled the early films of David Cronenberg and Ivan Reitman; it began distributing indies in 1995. CFP had ten releases in 1996, including *Heavy* and *The Young Poisoner's Handbook.*

First Look (Los Angeles, CA) was founded in 1993. This is the domestic distribution arm of Overseas Filmgroup, a foreign distributor. It has the potential to become a major indie. Films include *The Scent of Green Papaya, Party Girl* and *The Secret of Roan Inish.*

Goldwyn Entertainment (Los Angeles). (Samuel Goldwyn Entertainment) was a major indie for nearly two decades, releasing such art house favorites as *Stranger Than Paradise, Longtime Companion* and *Big Night.* Orion was a one-time mini-studio (like New Line and Gramercy) producing *Dances With Wolves,* among others. Through Orion Classics, it released such acquired indies as *Slacker* and *Mystery Train.* In 1997, both were purchased by MGM and disbanded. From the rubble, MGM formed Goldwyn Entertainment; its first release (in December 1997) was *Bent.* As of this writing, the future of the "new Goldwyn" is uncertain, but, with MGM's backing, it certainly has the potential to become a major indie in the near future.

LIVE Entertainment (Los Angeles, CA) has been a major video player for years. This company jumped into film distribution in 1994. Until recently, it was producing and releasing films through Orion (*The Substitute, Phat Beach*). Acquired titles include . . . *And God Spoke* and *Tree's Lounge.*

Seventh Art Releasing (Los Angeles, CA) was established in 1994. This company has acquired mostly European fare, but it also distributed the American-made films, *Risk* and *A Perfect Candidate.*

Strand Releasing (Santa Monica, CA) was founded in 1989. This company distributed a remarkable ten pictures in 1996 (in a very limited manner) and had its greatest success with *Stonewall*. Known as a champion of the marginal film (especially those with gay themes), Strand has released such titles as *Rhythm Thief*, *Hustler White* and *Grief*.

Trimark (Santa Monica, CA) was founded in 1990 as part of Vidmark (a major indie video distributor). This company acquires and develops edgy low-budget fare, as well as exploitable genre pictures like *Leprechaun*. In 1997, it released the prestigious success *Eve's Bayou*. Films in its library include *Federal Hill* and *Kicking and Screaming*.

Zeitgeist Films (New York) has handled—since 1988— innovative features with care, including *Poison*, *Silverlake Life* and *Manufacturing Consent*.

There are more small distributors which may go a year or more without acquiring a film, i.e., **Greycat**, **Roxie Releasing**, **Northern Arts**, **Unapix**, **First Run Features**. Some are new to distribution and don't yet have a significant track record, i.e., **FilmHaus**, **Artistic License**, **Legacy Releasing Corp**. Some handle primarily documentaries (i.e., **Tara**) or experimental media (i.e., **MK2 Productions**, **Panorama**). Others may concentrate on revivals or foreign films (i.e., **Kino**).

But any of these companies—or other, newer ones—may be open to your narrative feature. People like what they like. If they get excited, they may take you on (for little or no money up-front). If you're arranging a screening of your film, invite everyone. If you're sending out tapes, send them everywhere. And new distributors leap into the business every year, just as others disappear, so stay abreast of the latest developments.

It's ideal, of course, if several places fall in love with your film at first sight and a bidding war between major indies and studios begins. (These sorts of emotional battles are what create multi-million dollar festival sales.) But for our scenario, let's keep the romance more subdued. Let's say that two small companies are impressed by your film, which screened at IFFM, and now they're flirting with you before you go to the big 'dance in Park City. Before signing a contract, two questions should be preeminent:

1. Can you trust the distributor to pay what you're entitled to?

2. Will the distributor properly distribute and market your film?

The latter question is crucial: if your movie doesn't get into enough theaters (and the *right* theaters) or receive the right advertising, it will never make money and your directing career may screech to a halt. It will be hard for others to notice you and your movie if the distributor doesn't push your film hard.

The breadth of a distributor's commitment is measured by **P&A** (prints and advertising). This is a large up-front expense but it also can, virtually by itself, make you a celebrity. Warner Bros. put more than $6 million behind *Roger & Me*, instigating Michael Moore's career. In its first year, Fox Searchlight made a name for itself by pushing *The Brothers McMullen* to the tune of $10 million, and it simultaneously made a name for the film's director, Ed Burns. P&A commitments should be part of your negotiations and they should be written into your contract. When October bought the North American rights to *Lost Highway* for $5 million, it had to stipulate that it would also spend $5 million on P&A. More than $225,000 on P&A is good from a mini-indie distributor; more than $500,000, from a major indie; studios typically spend $4 million on even their smallest picture. These are initial commitments. If a movie takes off, most companies will be happy to funnel some of their profits back into more prints and advertising in order to generate greater profits.

So, you need to trust your distributor to do what's right for you, your pocketbook and your movie. The distributor's past record and its present reputation are the two best indicators. The company should be in a healthy financial situation; it should have leverage with exhibitors to collect money owed; its reputation for disseminating and marketing independent features should be impeccable. Find out what motion pictures a prospective company has released recently. Judge for yourself how well it has done. If possible, talk with producers from those films.

Not every small company has earned a reputation. If the only distributor calling you (or returning your calls) is a rookie or mini-

mini, you'll probably want to go for it anyway. Maybe such a company will push your motion picture that much harder because of its drive to stay afloat. Whatever the situation, hire a lawyer, spell *everything* out precisely in a contract and keep your eyes and ears open.

LEGALESE

After post-production, an independent filmmaker is usually flat broke (if not indebted); he is often weary, worried about his future and desperate to make any deal. Distribution companies are well aware of this. Therefore, many contracts end up heavily skewed in favor of the companies. Don't be a chump: never barter from a position of weakness.

As mentioned earlier, there are agents, managers and producer's reps who specifically handle indie pictures. If you're getting close to a deal, hire a representative with a stellar reputation. This person will take a percentage of your share, but he will fight for you on an equal playing field with the distributors. And remember, if you don't get paid, your representative doesn't either, and, the more you get paid, the more he does. The best representative can almost always negotiate for more cash and better conditions than you can for yourself, even subtracting his chunk. He'll also run his magnifying glass over the fine print and make sure you get what you think you're getting.

Buyers can make an **outright purchase** of all rights to your film. In this case, make sure you and your movie will be properly marketed and that the purchase price covers all the expenses you've incurred, plus a healthy profit.

The most common sales are **percentage deals** in which you share in the distributor's profits (if there are any). Typically, your return on domestic box office will be twenty-five percent to fifty percent of the distributor's return—after all costs are deducted for prints, marketing and shipping. Try to prevent the distributor from deducting legal expenses or overhead (i.e., staff and office expenses) or, like the studios, its books may never show a profit.

Most percentage deals will provide you with a **minimum guarantee** (also called an **advance**) on future profits. Of course, you'll want to maximize this up-front cash, especially because, after expenses, your film may never show a profit. Major independent distributors typically offer an advance in the six-figure range; smaller companies may not offer any up-front cash.

A twist on percentage deals is **first-dollar participation**, which means you'll collect a small percentage (say, eight percent) of all money returned to the distributor, beginning with the first dollar your film earns. You'll regularly get fairly small checks while the distributor pays off its expenses; if and when your film gets out of the red, you'll start receiving your full percentage (say, forty percent) of the profits. Because it seldom pays off as planned, this is a good deal only if it is <u>in addition</u> to a large advance —not in place of one.

A **service deal** is one in which you or, more likely, a video company, pays a distributor to release your film in theaters. *In the Soup, Killing Zoe, Gas Food Lodging* and *One False Move* were, to one degree or another, service deals. (Only the producers of *In the Soup* paid for theatrical distribution themselves.) Usually, service deals are set up by media conglomerates which use a theatrical run to increase the amount of their video and TV sales. Such arrangements can serve you well if effort (and money) are put into distribution (as with *Gas Food Lodging* and *One False Move*). That's a big "if." Service deals are a next-to-last resort—just above self-distribution.

Any contract for theatrical distribution should include:

- **Guaranteed commitment of marketing**. The more specific the P&A obligation, the better.

- **Right to regain distribution rights**, at no cost to you, if the company fails to release your film in the manner agreed to, within a certain period of time (typically, one or two years) or if the company files for bankruptcy.

- **Binding arbitration clause**. This legally ensures that all contractual disputes will be subject to mediation, with the winner reimbursed for legal fees and costs. Such a clause prevents disagreements from going to the courts where they can take years to untangle and where larger companies have the power and money to wear you down.

- **All warranties "to the best of your knowledge and belief"** rather than absolute. This legally protects you from much (but not all) liability.

- **Termination clause.** Such an item allows that if either party defaults (trapping the two of you in a bad marriage), the contract can be terminated.

- **The right to audit** the distributor's books. Also state in the contract that if you find a significant error, you'll be reimbursed for the cost of the audit.

While we're on the subject of contracts gone awry, a word of caution: retain legal possession of your negative. Negotiate to give the distributor a Lab-Access Letter only. This way, if there is a breach of contract, you can block the distributor's ability to make more prints. For similar reasons, try to retain the video master, stills and any artwork.

On the other hand, your distributor will probably want all of these things. It will usually write forfeiture of these items into the contract, thereby legally mandating that you comply. Called **deliverables**, if you don't already have them, getting these things can cost you time and money. Deliverables include:

- The **negative** of the completed film;

- The **videotape master;**

- **M&E audio tracks** for foreign sales;

- A **spotted dialogue list** (a list of the film's dialogue and action, in feet and frames—a major hassle and expense) and/or a **continuity script**. These are used with the M&E tracks for dubbing;

- A **Chain of Title** (documents tracing ownership of the film, from screenplay to distributor);

- Copies of all **clearances and releases** (for Errors & Omissions insurance);

- All **photos and slides;**

- **Press books;**

- **Biographies** of key personnel;

- Complete **cast and credits;**

  . . . and probably other items, specific to your film.

MISCELLANEOUS ANCILLARY

Before we get too far from contracts, let's discuss some ancillary rights that may or may not come into play. These are worth potentially as much as all other avenues of revenue combined. Studio movies sometimes clean up on these rights. And, while most indies don't find large success in this area, a few have broken through here. Therefore, negotiate to keep substantial percentages (twenty-five percent to sixty percent) of these rights, as sort of long-shot bets.

Story And Characters

This includes all additional rights to the screenplay and characters for remakes, sequels, stage plays, television programs, novelizations and published scripts. This category can bring surprise success for indies: *El Mariachi* gave birth to a studio sequel, 1995's *Desperado* (again written and directed by Robert Rodriguez); *Clerks* received a TV development deal; the documentary *Hoop Dreams* generated a bestselling book. Indie scripts do get published: Tarantino's work is on many a *cineaste*'s bookshelf. Finally, even plays and remakes come from independents: the micro-budgeted *The Little Shop of Horrors* (1960) was the basis for both a musical play and a film remake (which was based on the play). If author's rights are explored, the money is potentially huge.

Non-Theatrical

This category includes exhibiting a video version of your film on airplanes, ships, trains and in hotels. It also encompasses 16mm or 35mm screenings on military installations and at colleges, clubs, prisons . . . places you probably had never thought of. Potential earnings from non-theatrical venues often go uncollected because filmmakers don't pursue them. If you hold these rights, arrange a deal with a non-theatrical distributor. The possibility for airline exhibition is low because airlines usually have deals with the studios, but popular independent films can still generate tens of thousands of dollars from this category.

Merchandising

Action figures, T-shirts, games, posters, books, key chains, toilet seats . . . major studio releases sometimes make a fortune on merchandising rights. Chances are, coffee mugs sales will be limited for your indie effort, but, as with author's rights, you never know. With a good sales push, a quirky art film could reap success on this wide-playing field. "Making of" books are quite common. Among the directors who have penned them include Spike Lee (many times), Robert Rodriguez and Tom DiCillo (who wrote about his little-seen indie, *Living in Oblivion*). *Slacker* had a tie-in book that capitalized on the generational term and sold a respectable 20,000 copies. And there are more than a few *Reservoir Dogs* T-shirts and posters on college campuses. Develop your marketing ideas and prepare to hit the ground running.

Music

As the music is compiled for your movie, you'll know if there's a chance for a **soundtrack album**. If your film features a score of classic tracks or hot new bands, there may be an album and it could make as much as your film does in its entire theatrical run. On the other hand, original synthesizer compositions almost never get released.

A major distributor may have its own music company or an arrangement with one; it will want your soundtrack to be released in-house. In such a case, negotiate as large a percentage as you can. A small film company with no ties to the music business may cede the majority of these rights to the production; if so, shop your soundtrack to record companies. Begin your efforts with music companies whose artists are heard in your film. Without recognizable songs or performers and without a box-office hit, an album deal will be as difficult as selling a motion picture without recognizable stars or a festival buzz.

Music rights (master and publishing) are separate from soundtracks and they can be lucrative *(see "MUSIC: Prerecorded Song")*. These are rights to original songs. Publishing rights are generally held by the songwriter/composer, but master rights of original compositions are sometimes kept by the film production. If so, for the length of time you retain the rights, anyone who wants to use or cover these tunes will pay a fee that you set. (This is why you may have forked over $30,000 for thirty seconds of a pop song heard in the background of your movie.)

The Circuit

Before being distributed in theaters, your film will need an **MPAA rating** certificate. The cost of screening for the Motion Picture

Association of America will be more than $2,500, on an upwards sliding scale, depending on the size of the submitting company. This fee is almost always paid by the distributor. Sorry pornographers and "NC-17" artists, to advertise in most newspapers, and therefore to get projected onto most screens, your film will need to garner nothing harsher than an "R" rating.

To get things rolling, your releasing company may send you and your movie to a few festivals, hoping for positive press. Then your film will probably open in New York City and/or Los Angeles. On the other hand, in an effort to avoid colliding with the major press right out of the gate, it may premiere in a community perceived as having a strong "alternative" community, such as Seattle or Austin. If your film fills seats, it'll branch out to other cities.

This is the traditional way of distributing an art film; it's called **platforming**. Basically, this means you open in the biggest media markets and go to progressively smaller markets as the buzz spreads. Through the years, platforming has saved money on prints and marketing, and it has given small movies a chance to grow, allowing audiences to discover a motion picture months after its premiere.

Platforming is still a popular strategy, but these days the situation is more competitive. There are more movies, big and small, and they're vying for attention with cable TV, videos, computers, etc. If your picture doesn't generate great reviews and good business in New York or L.A., it may not travel any further. And if it does get onto a significant number of screens, holding time there can be difficult. Exhibitors often pull even successful indies to make room for product from bigger distributors. Theaters today rarely give small but growing films a chance to build an audience.

Some independent distributors no longer platform their movies. In today's crowded entertainment world, they'll put a film onto forty screens and blitz the media in an attempt to get noticed. Similar to the way studio flicks are released (only on a smaller scale), they'll target money into a national marketing campaign during prerelease days; if your movie catches fire during its first week, the company will open it even wider. If it doesn't catch fire, just like any Hollywood flop (only on a faster scale), it may all be over before you even know what happened.

Going "wide" for a festival-style indie translates into about 200 screens (as opposed to more than 2,000 for a studio flick). *The Brothers McMullen*, which opened in seven theaters, eventually played in more than 350 simultaneously, but this was an exception (Fox Searchlight, its new distributor, wanted to establish itself in the market). No matter how good the reviews and word of mouth are, most independent movies never make it onto more than sixty screens on a single Saturday night. Many now-legendary indies never even got close to this number. For example, *Reservoir Dogs* grossed only $2 million in domestic box office, even though it has brought in more than ten times that amount in foreign distribution, worldwide video distribution, TV and other ancillary markets.

No matter how your film is distributed, your job before and during its release is to work the press in conjunction with your distributor's publicity department (see "PUBLICITY, PART 2: Marketing"). Your life during this time will probably consist of keeping a phone glued to your ear, answering the same questions over and over, trying to generate word of mouth and planning tomorrow's blockbuster. Hope it goes on for months.

MONEY BACK

Once your film makes it onto screens, collecting your share of theatrical profits can present a major challenge. Money has to pass through a lot of hands before it can get to yours. Here's is a good case scenario:

1. A customer buys a ticket. $8.00

2. State and local sales taxes are deducted (approximately six percent). $7.52

3. The exhibitor typically keeps between 20% and 70%, depending on how its deal is structured. For a specialty film like yours, the theater will probably keep 60% to 70%, at least for the first few weeks of release. But, for this scenario, let's say it's only 55%. $3.38

4. Next, this money may go to a subdistributor who specializes in shipping films and auditing theaters. This company will also take a cut of the gross. But, for this example, let's say it goes directly to your distributor. $3.38

5. Your distributor deducts its expenses for prints and trailers, the fee for the MPAA rating and the costs for advertising, marketing and shipping. This comes right off the top. Usually, such costs are more than its percentage of the box office gross, meaning you and the distributor will see no profit. But, let's say your film has already covered the initial print and advertising costs so any additional expenses currently average out to a dollar per ticket. $2.38

6. In a 60/40 split between the distributor and the production (this is considered a good deal), a tally will be kept until your 40% totals more than your advance. If and when this happens, you'll start collecting your percentage. $.95

7. If your film still has debts, you'll have to pay them before you pocket any profit. But, let's say everybody got paid from your advance. So all investors (and anyone else with "points") share in the profits, one profit point equaling one percent. For our example, the total equity of these people is 25%. $.71

8. Subtract an estimated income tax of 20%. $.57

Fifty-seven cents from every full-priced ticket can be a significant sum, but your so-called sixty/forty split is actually netting you about seven percent of the box office take.

The good news is that as receipts go up, distribution costs decrease because word-of-mouth replaces much of the advertising and because the initial print-making expenses are behind you. Also, most theater/distributor deals are structured so that the longer a movie plays, the larger the distributor's share. So your percentage should increase dramatically if your film pulls in more than $4 million.

The bad news is that very few independents make anywhere near $4 million at the domestic box office. Less than one-third of the distributed films from Sundance 1996 made even $1 million in U.S. theaters. Only three made more than $4 million. And we're talking about Sundance veterans; these are supposedly the best indie films of the year. Approximately one independent movie in nine, of all those theatrically distributed, breaks the $1 million barrier at North American box offices. And even if your movie is that one in nine, your cut of $1 million (in the good case scenario explained previously) is $71,250. Hopefully, you received a minimum guarantee higher than that; so this means that you won't receive a royalty check during your film's stateside theatrical run.

But wait, the news gets worse. So far in our box office scenario we assume that everyone in it is completely honest. In the real world of film distribution, this is not always the case. Here's why:

- Theater employees can palm and resell untorn tickets, thus stealing from their employer (and you). This is less common in today's modern ticketing systems, but it still happens.

- Theaters can underreport sales. This can be guarded against by auditors (employed by distributors) who survey the books and compare them to ticket numbers from the beginning and end of a particular day. Auditors also sometimes stand outside a non-multiplex box office for a day or two and actually count, with a hand clicker, every person who buys a ticket.

- Theaters can fail to pay distributors. The bigger your release company, the more clout it will have and the faster it will probably collect its (and your) money. But, when dealing with struggling art houses, all distributors sometimes have trouble receiving their due.

- Your distributor can be dishonest. The most common schemes are: padding expenses; underreporting returns; charging to your film the cost of distributing other movies; and simply not paying you and not returning your calls.

Most exhibitors and distributors are honest people. But the art film scene can be tough. There aren't any *Jurassic Parks* to look forward to. The major indies might luck into a *sex, lies, and videotape* or *Pulp Fiction* to boost them to another level, but for smaller companies and smaller theater chains there's not much hope for a big payday. For them, independent cinema is a business of endless risks and meager profit margins. They may want to protect themselves by exaggerating expenses or understating returns. Or, they may go bankrupt before you receive your profits. *Protect yourself.* And make sure that your agent/manager/producer's rep is looking out for you—every step of the way. You're a flounder swimming in shark-infested waters: you gotta swim, but you also gotta keep your eyes open.

The best advice is to negotiate a large advance. It may be all the money you see from your film's theatrical run. Get some of the up-front cash that the filmmakers of *Swingers* ($5 million) and *Sling Blade* ($10 million) made; then you won't have to sweat about box-office numbers. Easier said than done, of course.

FOUR-WALLING

On the other end of the spectrum from large advances is truly independent distribution. Maverick director Henry Jaglom (*Eating*) owns his own releasing company, as did the late indie legend John Cassavetes (*Shadows*). Short of that, if you have a 35mm print and no interest from a distributing company, you can get it onto screens yourself. The process is called **four-walling** and it is as simple as renting a theater and its staff and selling tickets. You incur all advertising and marketing costs; you keep all the money from the ticket sales. The theater takes a healthy rental fee from you, and it keeps all the cash from concessions (a major source of revenue).

Popular in days gone by, when there were drive-ins and family-owned theaters, four-walling is rare today, mostly because of the scarcity of good, independently-owned screens. In the past decade, it has generated modest returns for certain niche films but four-walling is always a risky proposition. Usually, the money required to advertise and promote far outweighs the return from ticket sales. However, if your movie appeals to a certain audience segment and if you can get it into the right theaters and if you can find a way to market it cheaply and if word of mouth takes over, well, that's a lot of "ifs," but if all those "ifs" materialize, four-walling can work.

Here is a good example of four-walling that worked: Haile Gerima's *Sankofa* (1993) was an uncompromising feature about slavery that was rejected by festivals and distributors. It was then four-walled onto screens in African-American communities. The word was spread through fliers, filmmaker interviews in the black media and with the help of churches and activists. *Sankofa* went on to gross $3 million.

In 1996, a small distribution revolution took place: *omaha (the movie)* and Sundance veterans *Dade Town, Synthetic Pleasures* and *Paradise Lost* were among the movies put into theaters directly by their filmmakers. The documentary *Paradise Lost* steadily earned a box-office gross of more than $500,000—not bad for a documentary, especially when the production's share was 100 percent. Its filmmakers, Joe Berlinger and Bruce Sinofsky, also self-distributed the documentary *Brother's Keeper* in 1992. It made $1.5 million in theaters; their expenses were $250,000 (they also earned $700,000 on foreign sales and $100,000 on a video deal).

There have been a few movies that were successfully four-walled in a limited market and then were sold to distributors who took them into a wider release. This happened with *Slacker*, a smash hit in one theater in Austin before it was sold to Orion Classics. *Federal Hill* was opened by its filmmakers to enthusiastic crowds in Rhode Island before Trimark bought it.

Despite success stories, four-walling is not typically a method of getting rich and it requires a huge investment of work, time and passion. Still, if it's the only way your film can be seen by a paying audience, you may want to try it for a week, if only for the experience. If you turn a profit, try it for another week. Finding a willing theater can be a challenge. Inquire at art houses, college film societies and second-run venues. Forego the fee for an MPAA rating. Be frugal and creative with your marketing. Keep the independent spirit alive.

2G/FOREIGN

The entertainment market outside of North America is big and getting bigger. On average, studio films now make more in foreign theaters than they do in the United States and Canada. On a smaller scale, some U.S. independents do the same. The movies of Jim Jarmusch and Hal Hartley, for example, generate their biggest box office receipts in faraway lands. There are a lot of ticket buyers around the world, and viewers everywhere love American movies. Do not underestimate the ability of your little indie to pull in Deutsche marks, liras and yen.

THEATRICAL
The top foreign markets are Germany, England, Italy, Spain and France. These countries, like others worldwide, clamor loudest for big-budget action, big-budget flash and big-budget movie stars. Chances are, you don't have any of these elements. Still, European audiences can be receptive to small films, especially if they have a good North American run and/or play at a European festival. In fact, per screen, Europeans support our indies more than we do. The problem is, they currently have half as many screens per capita (Japan has one-sixth as many per capita).

If your film received foreign financing, it probably included foreign distribution rights as part of that deal.

For a particularly convoluted example of foreign financing and foreign distribution rights, the American production *Walking and Talking* (1996) was financed by a British production company (Zenith) with money obtained by pre-selling the rights to Italy (Mikado) and Germany (Pandora); British theatrical and video rights went to Electric Pictures & Polygram; British TV rights to *Channel Four*; and worldwide rights to a major French company (CiBy 2000) which, in turn, sold it to all other territories, including the U.S. (Miramax). Arranging all of this (plus various other ventures that fell through) took the producers no less than five years!

As mentioned, foreign rights are also sometimes sold during post-production to obtain finishing funds.

If you sign a domestic distribution deal, the company may or may not buy the foreign rights (assuming you still have them to sell). *The Incredibly True Adventures of Two Girls in Love* (1995) sold its domestic rights to Fine Line during post-production and its foreign rights to Miramax at Sundance. *Hurricane Streets* (1998) received more than $1 million from MGM/UA for its domestic rights and a similar amount from Mayfair for its foreign rights. Mixed deals like these are common, as are more complex ones in which different foreign distributors pick up a film for just their territory (country or group of countries). Don't pass up good international deals in order to hold on to all of your rights as one package. You can often make more money selling domestic and foreign rights separately.

If a big American company buys the foreign rights, it (or a foreign sales company working for it) will typically sell your film to various territories for a minimum guarantee, based on projected returns. For an indie, such guarantees will not be large but they do add up when totaled for all territories. If your film does better than the guarantee, the American company will share in the box-office profits. Depending on how your deal is set up, you, in turn, should get a percentage (say, twenty-five percent) of your distributor's guarantee and overages.

Studios and major indies can monitor the books of foreign exhibitors, but many smaller companies won't bother; it's just too difficult. They typically sell the negative outright to territories, take the money and forget about it. (If this is the case with your film, the distributor should send you a check so you can take the money and forget about it.)

If you maintain your foreign rights, selling them to the various territories is complicated. Try to use a **foreign sales agent** or company that specializes in these transactions. If you can interest one in your project, he will sell it around the world. Also, a producer's rep, manager or domestic agent may be able to handle this.

Warning: Many countries have Draconian import regulations that can prevent you from being paid for months or years (which may mean "never"). If at all possible, do not handle overseas transactions on your own.

Remember: You will need music and effects tracks that are separate from the dialogue track (see "SOUND EDITING: Mix") so that dialogue can be easily dubbed into non-English languages.

Foreign distributors may see your film at IFFM or at another major festival; they may read about it in a festival catalogue or hear about it through the distribution grapevine. If they're interested, they'll call you. If they're not calling, call them.

You may want to consider attending one of the foreign sales markets, such as Cannes (May); MIFED in Milan, Italy (October); or the American Film Market (AFM) in Los Angeles (March). Unfortunately, it can cost thousands of dollars to officially participate in these events—plus travel and hotel expenses. If you have a representative, he may attend as part of his job. If you don't, you can show up without an invitation and approach buyers outside of the official festivities; this is toughest at the AFM (which has a lot of security) and easiest at Cannes (a very open market). Also, you can send videotapes directly to various foreign companies.

When it comes to marketing, major movie stars travel the world on international press junkets; indie filmmakers, usually stay home and work the phones. Selling your film will depend on its U.S. box-office numbers, its attendance at foreign fests, any recognizable above-the-line names and good reviews. By the way, some American indies with overseas financing, like *Lost Highway*, open in Europe before premiering in the States.

Box-office numbers sometimes surprise. For example, a film like *Reservoir Dogs* or the latest from Jim Jarmusch can stagnate at the box office in the States, yet be a smash in France or Germany; meanwhile, *My Dinner with Andre* (directed by French legend Louis

Malle) was an art-house smash in the U.S. but a monumental flop overseas.

VIDEO

Most rules for foreign theatrical distribution rights apply to foreign video rights as well. The main difference is that, because of the cheaper overhead involved in video distribution, it's easier to make video sales. Again, these rights may be part of a bigger package or they may be sold individually; sometimes, a sale to a particular country will combine the film's theatrical and video rights. Japan, Great Britain and France are the largest foreign video markets.

You will need a broadcast-quality video master (without time coding), with a final sound edit and with all dialogue on a separate track for redubbing. Most countries require a PAL or SECAM master tape (a format incompatible with VHS).

If you still own some or all of your foreign video rights, you can sell them to each territory yourself or you can let a video distributor handle the sales and split the profits.

Don't agree to per-tape percentage deals because auditing overseas sales is nearly impossible and piracy runs rampant in foreign lands. Before sending tapes to distributors, you may want your lab to stamp "DEMO COPY" into the picture to reduce the chances of it being illegally copied.

If your film has not played in theaters, as always, action, violence, sex, and any recognizable name performer are at a premium. Unfortunately, they matter more than quality writing, directing, or acting. The promise of blood, sex, or a pseudo celebrity will be what gets plastered on the box cover, and video boxes drive foreign sales.

TELEVISION

Many American channels are available worldwide (see "DOMESTIC TV & BEYOND") and Canadian television can be handled through a U.S. syndicator. After that, foreign broadcasting becomes complicated. It's possible to make individual foreign TV deals before you have completed your film. *Roger & Me* sold its British TV rights at IFFM and *Slacker* struck a German TV deal there as well; the sales helped both works-in-progress get 35mm answer prints. Germany, with its government funding of indies, and England, with its artistic *Channel Four* (the station behind *Trainspotting*), are both good bets for early overseas dollars. Documentaries with universal topics (as opposed to ones that are distinctly American) may find the respect and financing they need in European television. Nonfiction works, such as *The Celluloid Closet* and *The Battle Over Citizen Kane*, both about cinema, were financed with foreign presales. You may have sold some rights as part of your foreign theatrical or video distribution deals. Typically, in such arrangements, your share of foreign TV revenue will be fifty percent.

Outside of Europe and Australia, most festival-quality indies will find television sales nearly nonexistent. Your best shot at such markets as Africa, South America and Asia will probably be if a syndicator or distributor places your film with a dozen or so better-known studio titles and sells them all in a single package.

Foreign television broadcasters learn about your film in the same way as distributors: through film markets, festivals, catalogues, the grapevine, your phone line. You can also consult a U.S. television syndicator or a foreign video distributor. You'll need a video master in the PAL or SECAM format with music, effects and dialogue on separate tracks.

27/DOMESTIC VIDEO

In the 1980s, video stores were a safety net for independent movies that failed to find theatrical distribution. You could almost always count on a video sale. Since then, the net has gotten smaller and smaller. Today, it's the size of a flyswatter.

Horror flicks with catchy titles and even catchier video sleeves can still make a little money by going straight to video. And there is still a premium on action, violence and sex, although even these tried-and-true favorites recently have had trouble squeezing onto crowded video shelves. And, of course, that recognizable name performer always helps (for American sales, "celebrity" expands to include the likes of Tonya Harding, Joey Buttafuco or any *Playboy* playmate). In 1995, there were 246 non-porn titles that went directly to video stores. More than seventy-five percent fit into the action, erotic-thriller or horror categories. Fewer than three percent were artistically made independents.

What about your film festival loser? If it was theatrically distributed, even if it only made it onto a few screens, you'll almost certainly get an American video deal. *Bad Lieutenant* (rated NC-17) pulled in $2 million domestically but stirred up enough controversy to equal that amount in video sales. The micro-budgeted *Straight Out of Brooklyn* has so far shipped 60,000 units (worth more than $1 million); *Killing Zoe*, a box-office dud, has racked up similar numbers. And *Reservoir Dogs* is a huge success on videotape, selling more than 150,000 copies to stores and consumers worldwide. (By the way, three of these successful video performers offer the promise of violence and the fourth, *Straight Out of Brooklyn*, has an all-black cast. Having a film that fits easily into a genre helps its sales.)

If your movie was not distributed theatrically, your road will be rough and winding. Without gore or a recognizable name, your best bet for a video sale is if your movie falls into a niche theme (i.e., gay, ethnic) or into a popular video genre (i.e., action, thriller, horror, children's). If it doesn't fit one of these conditions, you may have to hope that one of your now-unknown actors someday becomes a superstar.

For any video sale, you'll need a **broadcast-quality video master**, without time coding and with a final sound edit. This should be made at a telecine or on-line session and should include color correcting. Shop around for the best deal at film/video labs.

If you have a domestic theatrical distribution deal, that company probably holds the domestic video rights as well. There may be a profit-sharing split between the company and you, providing you with twenty percent to thirty-five percent of the net. In other contracts, your pay may be ten percent to twenty-five percent of the wholesale price of each tape sold. Often, the distributor will **cross-collateralize** video revenues with theatrical expenses so that if a film loses money on the big screen, it can recoup these losses from other markets (i.e., video, TV, foreign) before you participate in any profits. Try to limit this type of agreement.

Video distributors sometimes finance indies, in which case, video distribution is prearranged. This was the situation with *sex, lies, and videotape* (perhaps predestined by its title). Its $1.2 million budget came from RCA Columbia (domestic video) and Virgin (foreign video). (It has sold, remarkably, more than 200,000 videos.) Service deals are also frequently financed by video distributors, as was the case with *One False Move*.

Most of the major theatrical indie distributors and some of the mini indies have their own video distribution arms. If they don't, they might set up a deal with an established video company. Among the elite video distributors which handle non-studio films are **Vidmark, Republic, LIVE Entertainment, Hallmark Entertainment, Columbia TriStar Home Video** and **New Horizons.** All are based in the Los Angeles area.

If you still have control of your video rights, pitch your film to video labels (manufacturers). Send them a high-quality VHS dub from your master. If they license it, they'll sell it to a distributor who will sell it to chains, stores, customers, mail-order catalogues, etc., either by themselves or with the help of a larger company. Middlemen dilute your profits. With either a percentage of net profits or a gross royalty on sales, try to get an advance (this is uncommon for small pictures). As always, read the fine print.

Videos are priced for either sell-through or rental. Sell-through titles have a lower price tag ($10 to $30); rental titles are sold primarily to stores and chains in limited numbers and sport a larger price tag ($50 to $90). In a reversal from the 1980s, the vast majority of movies are now priced for sell-through. Rental-only films do tend to be small independents (as well as foreign language fare), but some indies have gone the sell-through route with good results. For example, all four of the video over-achievers mentioned previously (*Bad Lieutenant* and company) sell for between $14.95 and $19.95. Sometimes a film is released with a rental price but it is later slashed to the sell-through price.

You may be asked to get involved in marketing. Your involvement will primarily be through video trade publications or at events like the Video Software Dealers Association (held annually in Las Vegas). Big box-office numbers are the best selling point, but festival awards, positive reviews or an interesting behind-the-scenes story can help you pitch your film to retailers. Most of the sales will be to individual stores and local chains. The national chains, like Blockbuster, which has more than forty percent of the market, are the principal purveyors of a tiered system of buying: movies that do less than $5 million in domestic box office are called "B" titles, with B+, A- and A titles above them. Therefore, even popular indies get crowded out by loads of studio schlock.

Many theatrically distributed low-budget indies are not issued on **laser disc** or **DVD**, and motion pictures that don't make it into theaters are almost never distributed in these formats. However, if your film makes more than $2 million in domestic box office or if it receives significant attention for any reason, there may be a digital version. Most of the same rules for video rights apply to digital rights. (You gotta love the fact that films like *Pink Flamingos* or *I Spit on Your Grave* are available on digitally remastered discs and can be viewed on $5,000 home entertainment systems.)

As of this writing, the future looks digital. Although it's too soon to comment extensively on **DVD**, it has the potential to eclipse the VHS market in the first years of the next century.

Four-walling, so to speak, can be done with video distribution. If no label is interested in signing your movie, you can distribute a VHS version of it yourself. This is no way to get rich. Furthermore, with all the lab and manufacturing costs (i.e., master, dubs, video sleeves), as well as advertising, marketing and shipping expenses, it's most likely a way to lose money fast. But, if you have a specialty film and you already have a broadcast-quality master, you may be able to develop a strategy via mail order or by canvasing appropriate stores that will enable you to earn a small profit. You can get your film seen this way, but it's a lot of work for (most probably) scant monetary reward.

28/DOMESTIC TV & BEYOND

Although the medium of film has greater prestige than television, virtually everyone in the entertainment industry would like to have his work shown on TV eventually. This is because while getting your film seen by ten million people in theaters is considered very good ($65 million box office, factoring in reduced ticket prices), the worst-rated sitcom on a major network will have more than ten million viewers in a single night. And looking at a great theatrical run for an indie of perhaps 500,000 ticket buyers ($3.3 million box office), forget about it; even a lame cable channel can beat that in prime time. TV is important because it goes where the people are. By having your movie sent directly into living rooms, you can reach more people in one night than from your theatrical and video runs combined.

If you have a domestic theatrical distribution deal, chances are, television rights were included in the package and you'll probably receive a percentage of these sales. In the world of TV, with no prints to make or advertising to buy, the distributor's expenses are minimal and you should receive close to your full share (typically twenty-five percent to fifty percent) of the revenue.

If you still own all television rights, there are a multitude of potential markets where you can sell them (and more are surfacing all the time). But, as with video distribution, if your film was never released theatrically and you don't have any recognizable actors in your cast, your chances of selling to television are fairly low. And, the elements that worked in your favor in video distribution (i.e., sex and violence) can now hurt your chances for a TV sale. Your film title's recognizability is the most important element for any TV sale and this is primarily established through the advertising and publicity of a domestic theatrical run. If you have a popular product, television royalty checks may find their way into your mailbox from now to public domain. Your great-grandkids will be endorsing them. On the other hand, if you have an unknown, undistributed labor-of-love, you may have to hustle to get *anyone* to see your motion picture on a little screen.

It is standard practice that a feature film cannot be shown on most non-pay-per-view channels until a certain period has passed after its theatrical run and video distribution. Also, when your movie gets to non-pay channels, you (or the censors) may need to severely edit mature language, nudity, violence and drug use. Think of the future royalty checks as your creation is being eviscerated.

BASIC
This category includes everything your TV picks up via simple antenna. It also encompasses cable channels that do not require an additional fee.

Major Networks
Festival indie films aren't aired on network television.

Cable Channels
It is tough, but not impossible, for an independent film to be aired on a basic cable station, depending on the subject matter, name recognition of the actors and box-office success of the film.

Unless a particular company pays for exclusive rights, it is possible to sell your film to more than one channel at a time. Barring the possibility of your movie coming in a package deal from a major distributor (i.e., "Take this little indie and we'll throw in the next *Star Wars*"), in all likelihood, your picture will probably command the channel's lowest price.

Your work of art may need to be edited for television, as the saying goes, and it will certainly be chopped for commercial breaks.

Local
If your feature gets significant theatrical distribution and/or attention, it can be sold to **local network affiliates and independent stations**. The bigger the market, the more your film will earn.

Contact a television syndicator which sells to channels throughout the United States and Canada. Movies are often sold in large package deals (sometimes fifty or more films in a bundle). Of course, your movie may have to be edited and it will be cut for commercial breaks.

If your film was not theatrically distributed, don't despair. Local stations (especially in smaller communities) are sometimes interested in what a hometown kid has created; this may include the hometowns of your actors as well. Dust off your press kits and your pitch and approach the stations in your area and those of your lead actors.

PBS affiliates sometimes feature the work of regional film artists, usually unedited and uncut. A socially-conscious theme will increase your chances with PBS. If your film had government funding, a national PBS broadcast is probably included as part of the original financing deal. If not, contact your local affiliate.

Public access and community programming channels are also possibilities. They may be thrilled to feature the work of a local director or actor. Usually, there is no revenue. But it is a way (sometimes the only way) of getting people to see your creation in its uncut form. If it comes to this (and public access should be your last resort), check with local cable companies for free broadcast possibilities.

PREMIUM
The premium cable channels are the best small-screen venue for exhibiting your motion picture to a wide and discerning audience. Movies are shown uncut and unedited for any censor's concept of "adult language or content."

Movie & Entertainment Channels
HBO and **Cinemax** are sister stations. **Showtime** and **The Movie Channel** are sister stations, along with their new adopted sister, **FLIX**; these three are owned by media giant Viacom (which also owns Paramount Pictures, MTV, Blockbuster Video, Simon & Schuster, etc.). You can only sell to one set of stations (HBO/Cinemax or Showtime/Movie Channel/FLIX) on an exclusive basis, typically two to five years. The major movie channels have cloned themselves (i.e., HBO 1, HBO 2, HBO 3), and although they offer slightly

different programming, a sale to one (such as HBO/Cinemax) means they can broadcast your film on any of their clones.

Cinemax is the most indie-friendly of these options. It regularly features one independent movie, documentary or foreign film per week in its "Vanguard Cinema" showcase. Cinemax also has provided finishing funds to filmmakers.

The money is potentially good if your film is purchased for broadcast by any of these channels, but it will depend on when your movie airs and how many times it's shown. These factors, in turn, are based solely on the movie's domestic box-office gross and how recognizable the actors are (for example, HBO likes at least two "names" per picture). Often, quality independent films can't even get a slot while studio dreck plays over and over again in prime time. New channels, hungry for product, may be the best hope for marginal indies. For those of you who never played in theaters, sellable genres like action-adventure, sexy thriller and children's can squeeze onto these channels to fill up the non-prime-time hours.

Independent Film Networks

The indie channels are your best bet for significant airtime, whether you have an independent feature, documentary or short. These channels are found on some basic cable systems or they may be a pay service. Unfortunately, at present, many systems don't receive any of these, and precious few carry more than **Bravo**, the most popular of the three. Meager exposure limits their revenues which, in turn, limits your potential earnings.

Bravo is the older sister of **The Independent Film Channel (IFC)** and is usually a non-pay cable channel, and therefore it edits for television. But it edits to a lesser degree than networks, and thankfully, it does not cut for commercial breaks. It plays a variety of arts programming, including non-studio cinema.

The Independent Film Channel and **The Sundance Film Channel** are similar: they show your film, uncut and unedited and they are seeking the same type of product, including U.S. indie features, documentaries, foreign fare, shorts and experimental films. They usually buy the exclusive broadcast rights. Sundance is under the Viacom umbrella and may share titles with its sister companies; the IFC shares with Bravo. Both of these channels consider films which were never theatrically released, but the odds are certainly against you (with the exception of films that played at the Sundance Film Festival). Typical rates for a full-length feature that had a modest box office run are $10,000 to $40,000 for a two- or three-year exclusive term. The competition for popular indies may boost these prices.

Both Sundance and the IFC are flirting with the idea of financing feature films. The IFC was the first to step forward when it bankrolled *Gray's Anatomy* (1997), the Steven Soderbergh-directed film of Spalding Gray's monologue.

NEW OPTIONS
Technology is moving closer to the time when we'll be our own network executives: we'll each be able to schedule whatever movie or TV show or interactive media event we want to see—whenever we want to see it.

Pay-Per-View & Movies-On-Demand
Pay-per-view is a cable service that plays movies and special event programming at specific times and for a specific price. You pay a fee for each viewing. **Movies-on-demand** (or videos-on-demand) is a service in which you access a film whenever you want to see it; again, you pay per program. The possibilities for this type of technology are expanding.

Most movies exhibited this way are major studio films, soft-core pornography and higher profile independents (i.e., *The Brothers McMullen*). But every film will be a potential movie-on-demand in the future when your computer and your television will be working together (or, they will be one and the same). Fees range from a few thousand to a few hundred thousand.

Lease Access
Currently, this is the world of infomercials. But there are other possibilities here. As a film owner with TV rights, you can lease time on a cable station, screen your movie and edit in commercials. You'll make money by selling advertising time. When we have a few hundred channels to choose from, the opportunities to exploit lease access will be great . . . for better or for worse.

The Internet

You can screen your movie on the Net today. In fact, distributors currently are experimenting with the idea of screening a portion— or all—of a film via the Internet, hoping that a taste of the movie on a small screen will get people to see it on a big screen. The possibilities for advertising, promoting and broadcasting your film on computers are expanding every day. The low-budget indie *Party Girl* (1995) was screened on the Internet in its entirety before being released theatrically and, though only a few thousand people saw it on the Net—and in a tiny, low-resolution form—there was a national story about the event on "NBC News," garnering the film much-needed publicity. (Unfortunately, there was no happy ending for this story: *Party Girl* grossed less than $500,000 at domestic theaters.)

The onslaught of the information superhighway will be changing all the rules for video and television, and for theatrical distribution as well. With the click of a keystroke, consumers around the world will be able to activate state-of-the-art high-definition screens with digital sound, showing them any movie they wish to see, whenever they want to see it—right in their own living rooms. When this day arrives, video stores will be on their way out of business (DVD may help hasten their departure); television scheduling will be altered—or become obsolete; even theaters will be rocked to their foundations. How royalties will be paid when someone downloads your movie in Chicago or Bombay is a question yet to be answered. But one thing is for sure: independent film distribution will never be the same.

POST-POST-PRODUCTION

29/REFLECTION

Was it worth it? Was it worth spending all your money, working nonstop for eighteen months, perhaps going into debt, perhaps fretting a few years off your life? Was it really worth it?

In the best-case scenario, the answer will be an easy, "Yes." Ideally, you and your film will be the toast of Sundance. You signed a terrific distribution deal, saw your creation makes a huge splash at the box office, and you rode a wave of positive publicity. You signed a three-picture deal with a studio and you'll soon be starting pre-production on your $10 million sophomore effort.

In a more realistic good-case scenario, the answer will probably still be, "Yes." In a good case, your film went to one or two major festivals. It got a minor distribution deal that allowed you to break even and pay off your investors. You received some publicity in the indie scene and you're setting up financing to make another non-studio feature with a budget twice the size of the first.

But what if your film didn't receive theatrical distribution? (Most independent efforts don't.) What if your film didn't sell its foreign, video or television distribution rights? What if you didn't get any publicity? What if you have no picture deal? No future financing? Nothing lined up? Furthermore, what if, unlike before filming, you now have no money?

Well . . . you still have a movie. And that movie isn't going to disappear. Five years from now, you may be selling it to a pit stop on the information superhighway. And you undoubtedly learned a lot over the past year. And you made some new friends. Maybe the lack of money and recognition and the humbling experience of having your Hollywood hopes deferred will still outweigh the positives, but remember one more thing: you're a filmmaker now.

In the end, you have to ask yourself: would you be happier if you hadn't pursued your dream?

The low-budget film industry is an unforgiving, brutal racket. It sucks away time and money and energy like a vampire. But even if you're drained of all these things and even if you feel like you've been pummeled day in and day out in a year-long fight with your hands bound behind your back, you probably still, for better and for worse, can't wait to do it all over again, to capture another dream with light and mirrors and celluloid. Because you're a filmmaker.

APPENDIX

ORGANIZATIONS

AMERICAN FILM INTITUTE
2021 North Western Ave.
Los Angeles, CA 90027
213-856-7600
www.afionline.org

ASSOCIATION OF INDEPENDENT VIDEO AND FILMMAKERS
304 Hudson Street, 6th Fl.
New York, NY 10013
212-807-1400
www.virtualfilm.com/aivf

BLACK FILMMAKER'S FOUNDATION
670 Broadway, Suite 304
New York, NY 10012
212-253-1690
or
2049 Century Park East,
42nd Floor
Los Angeles, CA 90067
310-201-9579

DIRECTOR'S GUILD OF AMERICA (DGA)
7920 Sunset Blvd.
Los Angeles, CA 90046
310-289-2000
www.dga.org

FILM ARTS FOUNDATION
346 Ninth Street, 2nd Fl.
San Francisco, CA 94103
415-552-8760

FILMMAKER'S FOUNDATION
5820 Wilshire Blvd.
Suite 503
Los Angeles, CA 90036
213-937-9137
www.filmfound.org

IATSE, MPMO WEST COAST OFFICE
(crew unions)
13949 Ventura Blvd.
Suite 300
Sherman Oaks, CA 91423
818-905-8999

IFFCON (INTERNATIONAL FILM FINANCING CONFERENCE)
360 Ritch Street
San Francisco, CA 94107
415-281-9777

INDEPENDENT FEATURE PROJECT (IFP)

IFP EAST/IFFM
104 West 29th St., 12th Fl.
New York, NY 10001
212-465-8200
www.ifp.org

IFP MIDWEST
(Chicago)
312-587-1818

IFP NORTH
(Minneapolis)
612-338-0871

IFP SOUTH
(Miami)
305-461-3544

IFP WEST
1964 Westwood Blvd.
Suite 205
Los Angeles, CA 90025
310-475-4379

INTERNATIONAL DOCUMENTARY ASSOCIATION
1551 S. Robertson Blvd.
Suite 201
Los Angeles, CA 90035
310-284-8422

NATIONAL LATINO COMMUNICATIONS CENTER
3171 Los Feliz Blvd.
Suite 200
Los Angeles, CA 90039
213-663-8294

SCREEN ACTORS GUILD (SAG)
5757 Wilshire Blvd.
Los Angeles, CA 90036
213-954-1600
or
1515 Broadway, 44th Floor
New York, NY 10036
212-944-1030

THE SUNDANCE INSTITUTE
225 Santa Monica Blvd.
8th Fl.
Santa Monica, CA 90401
310-394-4662
cybermart.com/sundance/institute

**SUNDANCE FILM
FESTIVAL
INFORMATION**
P.O. Box 16450
Salt Lake City, Utah 84116
801-328-3456

WOMEN IN FILM
6464 Sunset Blvd. #530
Los Angeles, CA 90028
213-463-6040

**WRITER'S GUILD OF
AMERICA, WEST**
7000 W. 3rd Avenue
Los Angeles, CA 90048-
4329
213-951-4000
www.wga.org

PUBLICATIONS

BACKSTAGE
1515 Broadway, 14th Fl.
New York, NY 10036
212-764-7300

BACKSTAGE WEST
5055 Wilshire Blvd.
6th Fl.
Los Angeles, CA 90036

**CREATIVE INDUSTRY
HANDBOOK**
(annual business listings)
Graphics Marketing &
Management
3518 Cahuenga Blvd. West
Suite 205
Los Angeles, CA 90068
213-874-4181

DRAMA-LOGUE
1456 N. Gordon
Los Angeles, CA 90028
213-464-5079

FILM COMMENT
c/o Film Society of
Lincoln Center
70 Lincoln Center
New York, NY 10023-6595

**FILMMAKER
MAGAZINE**
110 West 57th Street
New York, NY 10019-3319
212-581-8080
www.filmmag.com

**THE HOLLYWOOD
REPORTER**
5055 Wilshire Blvd.
Los Angeles, CA 90036-
4396
213-525-2000

**INDEPENDENT FILM
AND VIDEO MONTHLY**
304 Hudon Street, 6th
Floor
New York, NY 10013
212-807-1400

INDIEWIRE
(daily Internet
independent film news)
www.filmmag.com/
indiewire

LA 411
(annual business listings)
7083 Hollywood Blvd.
Suite 501
Los Angeles, CA 90028
(213) 460-6304

**MOVIEMAKER
MAGAZINE**
1750 South Euclid
Pasadena, CA 91106
818-584-6766
www.moviemaker.com

PREMIERE
1633 Broadway
New York, NY 10019
212-767-5400

SHOOT DIRECTORY
(annual business listings)
5015 Broadway
New York, NY 10036
212-764-7300

VARIETY
5700 Wilshire Blvd.
Suite 120
Los Angeles, CA 90036
213-857-6600

BUSINESSES

**ALAN GORDON
ENTERPRISES**
(cameras)
1430 Cahuenga Blvd.
Los Angeles, CA 90028
213-466-4561

ARRIFLEX
(cameras)
600 N. Victory Blvd.
Burbank, CA 91502
818-841-7040

**BREAKDOWN
SERVICES, LTD.**
1120 South Robertson
Third Floor
Los Angeles, CA 90035
310-276-9166

**CFI (CONSOLIDATED
FILM LABORATORIES)**
(laboratory)
959 Seward Street
Los Angeles, CA 90038
213-960-7444

CREW CALL
(crew referrals)
28924 S. Western Avenue
San Pedro, CA 90275
310-547-1096

DELUXE LAB
(laboratory)
1377 N. Serrano Avenue
Los Angeles, CA 90027
213-462-6171

DRAMA BOOKSHOP
(film books)
723 Seventh Avenue
New York, NY 10019
212-944-0595

DUART FILM AND VIDEO
(laboratory)
245 West 55th Street
New York, NY 10019
212-757-4580 or
800 52-DUART

ENTERPRISE PRINTERS & STATIONERS
(production forms)
7401 Sunset Blvd.
Los Angeles, CA 90046
213-876-3530

FOTO-KEM/FOTO-TRONICS
(laboratory)
2800 W. Olive Avenue
Burbank, CA 91505
818-846-3103

FUJI
(film stock)
1141 N. Highland Avenue
Los Angeles, CA 90038
800-326-08000

KODAK
(film stock)
800-621-FILM

LONE EAGLE PUBLISHING
(film books, directories and online service)
2337 Roscomare Road
Suite 9
Los Angeles, CA 90077
310-471-8066
www.loneeagle.com

MICHAEL WIESE PRODUCTIONS
(film books)
11288 Ventura Blvd.
Suite 821
Studio City, CA 91604
818-379-8799

NICHOL MOON ENTERTAINMENT
(production services)
2604 Devita Place
Los Angeles, CA 90046
213-876-8193
800-550-6342

PANAVISION
(cameras)
6219 De Soto Avenue
Woodland Hills, CA 91367
818-316-1000

SAMUEL FRENCH BOOK STORE
(film books)
7623 Sunset Blvd.
Hollywood, CA 90046
213-876-0570
800-8-ACT-NOW

THE SHOOTING GALLERY
(production services)
145 6th Avenue, 7th Floor
New York, NY 10013

STUDIO FILM TAPE
(film stock)
1215 N. Highland
Los Angele, CA 90038
213-466-8101
or
630 Ninth Avenue
New York, NY 10036
800-444-9330

THE WRITER'S COMPUTER STORE
(screenwriting and budgeting programs)
11317 Santa Monica Blvd.
Los Angeles, CA 90025-3118
310-479-7774
www.writercomputer.com

INDEX

THE HOLLYWOOD JOB HUNTER'S SURVIVAL GUIDE, $18.95
Insider's advice on getting that all important first job in the entertainment industry and keeping it.

BREAKING & ENTERING: Land Your First Job In Film Production, $17.95
Invaluable field guide to surviving the day-to-day rigors of a Hollywood movie set.

THE FILM EDITING ROOM HANDBOOK, 3rd Edition, $24.95
This semi-technical illustrated book covers the editing process from pre-production through post-production.

FILM SCHEDULING, $22.95
Details step-by-step how to create a professional production board & shooting schedule, shot-by-shot, day-by-day.

FILM BUDGETING, $22.95
Details the steps of converting a motion picture schedule to a professional motion picture budget.

FILM SCHEDULING/FILM BUDGETING WORKBOOK, $19.95
A complete do-it-yourself workbook companion to Film Scheduling and Film Budgeting.

MOVIE PRODUCTION AND BUDGET FORMS, $19.95
Tear-out professional forms, including call sheets, production report, deal memos, budget form and more.

FILM DIRECTING: Killer Style & Cutting Edge Technique, $22.95
For the director skilled in basic directing techniques who wants advice to achieve the emotional and visual impact demanded by today's motion picture industry.

ANNUAL FILM AND TV CREDIT & CONTACT DIRECTORIES
Please call for titles and availability. All directories are available online in a password subscription database

ABOUT THE AUTHOR

Greg Merritt has an MFA from The American Film Institute. He wrote, directed and produced an independent feature entitled, *Show and Tell*. He has worked on numerous film projects, won screenwriting awards, and optioned several scripts currently in development. He is also the author of a forthcoming comprehensive istory of American Independent Cinema.

Mr. Merritt can be reached regarding film consultations (development through distribution) and script critiques at P.O. Box 4404, Culver City, CA 90231-4404.